High Performance Thinking Skills

S.P. Reid

Published by **Permillion**

a division of

Spring Business Innovation Ltd.
Keepers Lodge, Main Street, Wysall
Nottingham, Nottinghamshire
NG12 5QS England

Telephone +44 (0)1509 880096
Email ask@permillion.com

10-ISBN: 0 9552700 0 6
13-ISBN: 978 0 9552700 0 0

Cover Design in collaboration with re:design, http://www.redesign.gb.com

Copy-editing: Marie Shields, htttp://www.marieshields.com

Typesetting by Pantek Arts Ltd., Maidstone, Kent

The three illustrations involving the sharks, the dragon and the frame enclosing two people were drafted by S. P. Reid and taken to final art form by Rich Skipworth, http://www.richskipworth.co.uk

The Polarity Map® and trade marks Multarities™ and Polarity Management™ are used with the permission of Barry Johnson.

Printed by Bell & Bain Ltd., Glasgow

Origins of This Work

The majority of the ideas and concepts outlined here have at some stage since 1995 been either created, adapted or discovered during the course of my consulting work, usually in response to a pressing need to help people to understand something complex or hidden. Alternatively, some ideas have emerged from a willingness to learn from difficult personal experience. Ideas that have evolved from personal experience have then been informally checked and tested out with other people to see if they are transferable and practical. My first book **How to Think** was published by Pearson Education in 2001. This book offers 82 examples of the many models I work with.

How to Get the Best Out of This Book

I do not recommend you attempt to read this book from cover to cover. There are more than 80 modules in this book. Instead use the next few pages and the 'In a Hurry' Section to decide which modules you want to explore. If you adopt a selective approach what you read will be relevant and will be more likely to help you. Additional materials will be loaded onto the web site in support of individual modules.

See **http://www.spreid.com**. The author also welcomes direct feedback and suggestions. Email: info@spreid.com

Conventions

Currencies. This book will be sold in a variety of countries around the world. With this in mind, I have used the American dollar ($) as a globally recognised currency.

Gender. For ease of reading I have avoided using the term 'he or she' unless it clearly does not make sense to do so. 'He' and 'she' have been used in alternate modules to denote persons of either gender.

About the Author

The majority of Stephen Reid's work is with senior managers in the UK, Europe and beyond. His work is focused on developing improved performance by providing new ways of thinking and behaving. Projects have included strategy formulation, improved leadership, high performance teams and creativity. He also works occasionally as a mentor. Stephen is currently interested in what he describes as 'a performance philosophy'.

Stephen is an entertaining and engaging public speaker on subjects that require new ways of thinking and behaving in a complicated world. He has lived and worked in a variety of countries. He has a strong commercial background, having successfully fulfilled roles as a country manager, general manager and director, working for large, multinational health-care companies.

In addition to his consulting work, Stephen has delivered workshops as an associate at The British Chartered Institute of Marketing, The Strategic Planning Society, The ACCA, and The National School of Government at Ascot, England, and in the past as an occasional guest lecturer at Ashridge Management College in England.

Stephen is also an amateur painter.

Previous Publications:

How to Think, *Building Mental Muscle*. Reprinted three times in English, 2002 to 2006. Also published in three other languages.

Web site: **http://www.spreid.com**
Contact: info@spreid.com

Contents: Overview

If you are *in a hurry,* see these fast-track reading guidelines. Specific modules are proposed as recommended reading for a variety of subjects.

Contents

Contents

Introduction

How to Use This Book

Don't read it cover to cover. *Make it personal.*

First look at the four mindscapes or territories, starting on the next page. Then estimate 'where you are now' in terms of the way you use your mind. You will get the best out of this book by choosing individual modules that you believe are most likely to be of help. At the back of the book is a brief section entitled **'In a Hurry'** that provides a quick guide to recommended module numbers according to particular subjects. I do not recommend you read my book from cover to cover because that would not fit your personal needs. However, I do hope you will find the book a helpful friend to be referred to over the years.

When you consider where you believe you are within the four territories outlined below, please remember that these are crude estimations and probably overlap. Keep in mind that the aim of personal improvement is not necessarily to seek to get to a different territory. Instead, concentrate first on being as good as you can possibly be within your present terrain. Only then should you contemplate what you will do next. Build yourself up on solid foundations.

About Your Travel Plan

Any journey involves a starting point and a destination. Most people know where Mount Everest is, but not everyone wishes to climb all the way to the top or to stay too long at its summit.

Look at the four different territories or mindscapes that you may wish to travel through on your way to self-improvement. Each of the four territories is **different in some way, but** the more difficult territories are **not** necessarily the best places to be. What matters the most on a self-improvement journey is to be the best you can be within the mental territory that fulfils your needs the most.

Where You Are

You can exercise and 'work out' to make your muscles stronger. The same is true for your mental muscles. **You can upgrade, nip and tuck your own mind – no scalpels required!** We are all born with the special gifts of learning AND adaptability. These gifts mean that whatever happens, you can always improve. Therefore if you want to achieve a higher level of personal performance by building up your

The four territories represent realms of increasing difficulty.

mental muscle, you will need some kind of milestones or benchmarks. You'll need to estimate where you are now and where you want to get to. Given the four territories below – where are you now? Would your closest friends agree?

The First Territory – A Clear Immediate View

In this territory, people adopt almost exclusively one of just two major thinking paths as their primary thinking/behaving mode. In both cases, self-awareness levels are relatively low.

Path 1. People who adhere almost totally to this path understand basic logic – cause and effect. Thinking is linear and often involves just one step. Focus and action are their priorities. All or most decisions are seen in terms of either/or. Their orientation is characterised by statements that involve words such as 'must', 'should' and 'always'. They frequently view the world as a place comprised of absolutes.

Alternatively, there are a few people who prefer **Path 2**. They prefer a loose, open-minded, floating existence, but are often almost totally incapable of making focused decisions. They may come up with truly original ideas, but then move on quickly to something new as the novelty wears off. People who are stuck with this pattern of thinking might be described as a 'scatterbrained' or 'dippy'. They may be creative, but are often unable to capitalise on their work unaided.

Breaking Out of the First Territory

This involves gaining ability in using 'the other' less-used thinking style when appropriate. For most people in the West, this involves being able to usefully employ creative (divergent or 'open') thinking. For those people who live scatterbrained, dippy lifestyles, more 'focused' (convergent) thinking and routine is their remedy.

The Second Territory – Light Fog and Uncertain Ground

People at this level have modest capability within each of the two major thinking paths and also possess and use a few mental models and tools. They have learned a very important lesson and now possess a better understanding of the idea of *the relative* as opposed to *the absolute* nature of issues. Consequently, they have developed a low to moderate tolerance for ambiguity and uncertainty. Self-awareness is low to moderate, occasionally during or after the fact. There is some ability to reflect, and then act based upon revised thinking.

Breaking Out of the Second Territory

This involves honing both focused and creative thinking skills. Especially necessary is an even higher tolerance for ambiguity. Personal confidence building is important, alongside rising self-awareness. As a result of the very high levels of ambiguity in the third and fourth territories, the majority of people do not feel comfortable there. Some people may make occasional forays into these more difficult terrains and then retreat to a level at which they feel more comfortable. In order to cope at the more demanding levels, you will need an ability to live with and deal with sustained ambiguity, high uncertainty and lots of contradictions. Access to more mental tools helps.

The Third Territory – Hills of Shale, Thick Fog and Swamps

At this level, alternative ways of thinking are fully integrated. People operating in the third territory can very quickly visualise and articulate complex issues. They can just as quickly synthesise new AND realistic ideas, focusing on the key issues. Such people have a moderate to high tolerance for ambiguity. They also have moderate to high levels of self-awareness and associated self-confidence. They are capable of routinely living with and dealing effectively with dilemmas and contradictions. Individuals with this level of skill can also live with two competing ideas and see each as valid and viable at the same time. A person at this level might be capable of taking and answering more than one question at a time. They have many mental models and tools at their disposal, are capable of original synthesis, and by implication can independently generate new mental tools and filters as required.

Breaking Out of the Third Territory

This involves improving tolerance for self and others, resolving deep or old inner personal conflicts, and experiencing alternative philosophies so a reasoned choice can be made. It involves holding authentic, well-considered beliefs and behaving humanely in accordance with these.

The Fourth Territory – Mountain Tops and Clouds

People operating at this level have all the attributes of territory three, but also operate with very high levels of self-awareness (always on). They have articulated and follow well-developed personal philosophies. They are capable of adjusting their states of 'being'. They demonstrate masterful thought and timely action with seeming ease.

Improvements at Any Level

Within each territory there are variables that can be improved through practice and learning, regarding:

- speed of processing (fast or slow)
- depth, range, quality and volume of knowledge held (reading, travelling, experiencing and learning)
- our inner self, our inner conflicts and feelings
- tolerance for ambiguity, uncertainty and therefore risk
- energy motivation and the emotions
- clarity as to what is real and what is an illusion
- state of being – anxiety/happiness/well-being/calm

For example, you may choose to operate in the first territory and have exceptional skills in influencing other people who share your view of the world. You could work on depth and breadth and gain a truly encyclopaedic knowledge of a chosen subject and remain comfortable operating at your chosen level. In this respect, you will have upgraded your mental muscle. To re-affirm, the aim of your development need NOT necessarily be to reach the higher ground, because that approach offers no guarantee of fulfilment or happiness. There are many directions in which you can stretch, build and improve. Aim to be the best at the level at which you feel most proficient **and** fulfilled. The journey need not all be upward.

As a general guideline, should you wish to excel you should do the following:

- look beyond rational logic
- learn alternative thinking skills and employ lots of different mental models
- recognise the connection and relative connections between things
- value creativity AND focus
- and especially, learn how to deal with ambiguity

But *the* single most important gateway to higher personal performance is:

- **self-awareness**

Whatever you choose to do, I also recommend you build up your social skills so that you can bring your thoughts and ideas into action through other people. In dealing with work and home life we also have to face several complexities:

- our relationships with other people
- the way we deal with what we experience (in terms of how we process our thoughts and then act) which directly or indirectly often involves other people

Look after your energy and nurture a positive philosophy and you will thrive. Guidelines on these topics are to be found within this book.

I'd be pleased to hear how you get on with my book. You can contact me via the web site **http://www.spreid.com**

Territory One

A Clear Immediate View

Mental Muscle Building: The Warm-up

Exercise your mind by considering how you might go about improving your personal performance based on how you think. Let's start with some break-out ideas. A step up from territory one involves increasing **the range** of available mental skills and NOT limiting yourself to the use of just one major thinking pattern.

Breaking the frame and moving up from territory one involves increasing your thinking skills using

either

more creative thinking (modules 2 to 9)

or

more logical thinking (modules 10 to 13).

In the modules that follow, I will first assume your primary skill is that of a logical thinker and immediately provide a number of tools that will help you build up your creative thinking ability. We will then look at how we might upgrade your logical thinking skills.

This next exercise is good fun.

Module 1

Prior Knowledge Can Get in the Way

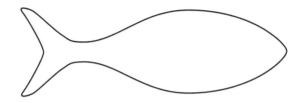

Humans have an ability to take existing information and make predictions as to what might happen next or what the answer to a question *could be*. Our skill in doing this can help us in some situations, but can also hold us back in others.

Exercise

Please try this exercise. It will show you how you perceive new information, but most of all it's fun to do. First draw a fish outline. If this is your book, use the image above. Draw in the fins on the picture. Most fish have eyes. Draw in the eyes.

Now draw in the mouth and the gills. Sound travels better in water than in air. Please draw in the fish's ears. Yes, fish really do have ears! If you eat fish, you can tell people you have eaten fish ears! (The correct answer is given at the end of this module.)

What We See

When faced with new challenges or new questions such as, 'Where are those fish ears?' we tend to try to predict, even if we do not actually know the answer. The real problem is, what we know gets in the way of what we do not know. One of several boundaries to our ability to 'see' is prior knowledge, coupled with our tendency to predict.

What to Do

When faced with novel challenges your best reaction would be to fight your instinct to guess or predict. Declare your lack of knowledge regarding the novelty in an honest and open way. This creates permission for others to look at the issue with a more open mind.

Why This Is Important

Sometimes personal pride or a wish to avoid looking stupid tempts us to say or do the wrong thing. An early clear admission saves wasted time and effort. It is particularly important for people in authority to do this. Admitting you do not know something demonstrates that you are a real human being, fallible and therefore all the more authentic.

TIPS

- Say you don't know when you don't know. It can be liberating and much more productive sometimes to start from nothing.
- Ask someone really naive what he thinks and what ideas he has concerning a new subject.

Uses

For fun as a team game and in illustrating how a little knowledge can be a dangerous thing.

Answer:

A fish has ears that run down both sides of its body. Fish hear sound through a series of small pits embedded in 'the lateral line'. You can see this as a horizontal mid-line of darker flesh running from behind the gills to close to the tail fin.

Upgrade Your Models and Tools : Creativity

Module 2

The Creative Edge: What It Is and How You Get It

Creativity Guidelines: Five Different Creativity Tools

Creativity is not a skill to be absorbed just by reading. You cannot learn how to ride a bicycle or to play soccer only by reading a book; you have to learn to kick the ball or mount the bicycle and have a go. Then lots of practice improves performance. The same is true of creative skills. You must have a go. If we don't routinely exercise our creative mental muscles, our minds and our lives will grow flabby.

General Creativity Guidelines

The creative thinking tools that follow can be used either by individuals or groups. Sparks can fly when several minds work together. Where possible, you will find you get better results when you work creatively with friends or colleagues.

What We See

In the last decade, creativity has moved from the fringe to the general mainstream, and creativity courses can be found in a variety of businesses and organisations. However, the teaching of alternative thinking on a wider platform than just creativity skills still has some considerable way to go before we can say that these are a mainstream part of our everyday education.

What to Do

Try several of the different exercises suggested below. There are many more creative thinking tools available, so find what works best for you. Where possible, encourage people with **diverse backgrounds** to be members of creativity workshops.

Why These Skills Are Important

At a minimum level, we require at least a little imagination in order to develop useful estimates and predictions. At a slightly higher level, creative thinking helps us to generate ideas and gain a wider perception of what may become possible. It is smart to have a variety of tools in your kit bag. The following modules may help you in a variety of different situations.

TIPS

With any exercise:

- You may feel awkward, even frustrated, but try to maintain this feeling of 'tension' as a useful tool to stimulate your mind. If you do feel uncomfortable do not worry, this feeling of tension is normal when you are learning without boundaries.

- Your raised attention levels, stimulated by ambiguity and tension, will demand a lot of energy, so expect to feel tired after any creativity exercise.

- Adjust your expectations. You are more likely to develop partial answers or clues. Phrases such as, 'We believe the answer... may have something to do with... or may possibly involve...' can be helpful.

- As you are making progress creating ideas, try to retain a high novelty value. Weak ideas will be easily copied or predicted. If your answers are sounding too conventional, try to extract more novelty by employing the more bizarre elements.

- Be brave and prepared to be at least a little outrageous!

- If you train individuals, then be aware that when they return to work in a team the group may dilute their new ways of thinking. When whole teams join together to learn alternative thinking skills any new skills are much more likely to be recognised and accepted.

Uses

Many and varied. New product, new service, new policy development. In negotiation, problem-solving and strategic change. We can be creative about how we please our friends and partners. Generating new ideas is a multi-billion dollar industry.

Module 3

Creativity Tool: Random Words

From a great distance and usually from a bizarre viewpoint, new ideas and solutions to our problems can be created. Word play can take us on a playful journey far away from the confines of present thinking. Distance can be useful in helping us to depart from everyday perceptions of reality. This is one of those activities that has to be experienced. When I say to people you can be creative using a dictionary, I always get some cynical looks or the laughter of disbelief.

After such an exercise people are almost always amazed.

What We See

The method works when we ask our minds to connect a strange idea with a real problem. The ambiguity this creates will, given a little encouragement, drive our subconscious minds into overdrive to produce original new ideas and solutions. This works well with individuals and with mixed groups of people. This method is low on structure and can be quite liberating. A small number of people who live by the rules may find the anarchy and chaos of this method a little unsettling, simply because it is different AND because it can produce results despite their misgivings. This last aspect needs to be managed properly.

What to Do

State the problem simply, then forget it for 20 minutes or so. Pick at random three words from a small pocket dictionary. Write down each of these three words onto unlined paper. For each word, spread your thinking by putting on paper whatever each word stimulates.

Continue by extending the best words by free association and adding new words or images, either working as a group or alone. Spend approximately 20 minutes having fun with the process.

- Do not look for any particular answers to the problem at this stage.
- Play with anything that stimulates a sense of fun.
- Try not to dwell on which words or images to write up.
- Move quickly and freely.
- Indulge yourself, feel free to laugh and to enjoy what you are doing!

After 20 minutes, if working in a group of five or six people, each person picks a powerful suggestive word or image from the output of the whole group. People should choose words that provoke some feeling or sensation! If you are working alone, select any five words that appeal to you. Allocate your choice(s) to a big clean space.

8

Idea Development

This is a contradictory place of 'playful responsibility'. You can still play, but pragmatic new ideas will be expected at this stage.

Select one powerful word to work on. Start to 'force' this word onto the issue to which you need an answer. This stage is the really demanding part. Do not be tempted to rush back into conventional solutions. What do your path or the current words suggest? This step may involve a little further extension of the words, but remember the goal now is to force out several useful connections, however abstract.

'Play' with a chosen word until you get bored or you or your team have exhausted its potential. Then pick another of your chosen words to connect to your original problem and repeat the process. See what emerges.

TIPS

- Do not expect complete, ready-made solutions. Great ideas are born drowning. They will need to be built up and improved.
- Expect to get partial suggestive answers – clues as to where to go next.
- Do not expect the process to work on schedule. This is a non-linear process.
- You might get a lot of answers, many of them unexpected.
- Does the pattern of the answers suggest anything new?
- Great ideas come attached to an emotional reaction. Look for 'aha!' moments – what did you realise?

Uses

Product development and strategic planning. Also, long before I set out to teach this particular method, in my role as a country manager I used this particular technique when there was no one else with whom I could begin an exploratory conversation. Random words, plucked from a dictionary, would occasionally help to surface useful questions in my mind.

Next Steps

Try the method in a safe low-impact context – for example, make it a game and show your children.

Module 4

Creativity Tool: Assumption-busting

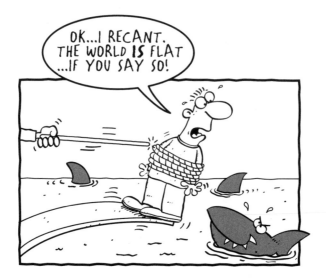

Most people believe that their reality is comprised of and ring-fenced by what they regard as facts or truths. We continue to think of these as valid FIXED truths, when in fact many of our 'truths' are often founded on assumptions. A game of assumption-busting can be used as a way of escaping our present view of reality and as a way of generating new ideas.

Examples: We assume we need to attend work or our education during conventional hours, that there will always be oil, that cars need wheels, that paper money has real value or that the internet will always be there.

What We See

Our interpretation of the world as relatively fixed can act as a barrier to new learning; therefore, a direct attack on what we assume to be 'true' about a given situation can produce useful insights.

What to Do

Define the problem or the opportunity simply. Develop a list of as many assumptions as you can think of, then forget the currently accepted truth for 20 minutes or so.

Select just a few assumptions you suspect could be interesting and then 'bust' them up. Assumptions can be corrupted by creating a lie. The bigger or more bizarre the lie, the better.

Creative displacement or whopping great lies can be produced in several ways. For example, parts of the assumption can be made bigger, smaller, fewer, multiple or non-existent – by flipping them over to mean something else, by reversing roles, by exaggeration or by subtraction of part or all of the assumption. Meaning can be distorted by making the assumption true for only a very limited or a very long time. For example, if you were looking at education, you might consider that each person gets only one day of formal tuition per year, but anywhere and in any manner. Alternatively, true meaning can be distorted by making the assumption true but only for a different quantity or quality.

A few of the lies or distortions will look like the basis of a stimulating discussion; the rest will be nonsense. Pick the more bizarre corruptions of 'the truth' or the ones you like best. If you are working alone or in a group decide on the three best distortions and then deal with each one separately., Treat each 'lie' as if it were to become real. Start a conversation in which you imagine the effects of transforming the lie into a new reality. The conversation usually gathers pace, so everyone should try to write some notes on developments. See where the lie leads. Usually the more bizarre ideas can go through several steps until they are very funny or surreal. Along the way you or the group should treat each suggestion as absolutely real and should attempt to imagine what it would mean in practical terms to really implement each bizarre idea. Extend the consequences as widely as possible and see what happens.

Do not worry if the ideas are incomplete, you can build them up later.

When you have had enough fun with the distortions of current assumptions you should be a great distance from reality.

After 20 minutes of play with a chosen lie, it's time to look for interesting lessons that may prove useful in the real world. Force your mind to come to useful conclusions about what can be done in the real world using only the best parts of the ideas within the bizarre realities you have generated.

Finally, consider what could be added, reinforced or combined to produce several more improved ideas.

TIPS

- The simpler, obvious distortions tend not to lead anywhere useful. Therefore, push the boundaries and use the outrageous or bizarre ideas first. To get into this technique it has to be fun!
- It is VERY important that at the end of the session you destroy any notes that no longer serve a purpose, simply because no one from outside the process would be able to make a reasonable interpretation of these.
- In a presentation, share only the conclusions. It is not wise to disclose the route taken.

Uses

I have found this tool useful for a variety of subjects. Since our deeper assumptions form part of our 'rules for life', I find that the assumption-busting technique lends itself to creating new policies. On more than one occasion, the 'lies' we generated turned out to be close to the truth.

Next Steps

Try the method in a safe, low-impact context – for example, use it to write an imaginative story or as part of your own thinking through a new policy.

Module 5

Creativity Tool: Rich Pictures

Groups of people carry a lot of valuable information in their heads. Getting people to express all or most of this valuable information productively in a short space of time can be difficult. Drawing images helps to surface ideas in our minds that are struggling to be heard. Often groups may share unspoken experiences that, once revealed, quickly produce a useful, informative map that describes the path from a difficult past to a better future.

What We See

This is quite simple and again involves playing with tacit material from the subconscious. This is applied 'doodling', but on a really big scale! You need as big a piece of paper as possible plus lots of colouring materials, objects, magazines and accessories. Most people assume they cannot draw and therefore avoid drawing. Yet images reside in their minds that explain complex issues. Once people recognise that the process is not competitive and that people's drawing skills are mostly of the same level, the process opens up and is productive.

Rich pictures have been used to get people with a traumatic past to vent and express repressed experiences in a safe environment. I have seen groups similarly come to the realisation that they share a common hidden problem that needs to be addressed.

What to Do

This is easy to do. Use lots of paper. Overlap the paper to stop people drawing on a wall. Use lots of colour. Shapes are allowed but words are to be discouraged. Crayons are good. Use the paper as if there are three time zones. Start with the present on the left-hand third of the paper and the distant future on the right-hand third. The space in the middle connects the two and represents a time of transition. In the beginning, allocate people to work on the left or the right. After a while, ask people to switch places. Then ask everyone to create transition drawings in the middle space.

When the energy is used up, get the groups to explain their pictures and then get them to compare imagery. Look for common themes. Consider what is included and what is missing.

TIPS

- Avoid marker pens that 'strike through' the paper and mark the walls.
- Take a digital camera to capture results for later.

Uses

This tool is quite good for doing a transitions map for people on a change journey. It's also good for exposing deeper unspoken concerns. Use as part of a strategic planning exercise.

Next Steps

Again, this is good fun to try out in a low-impact environment initially. Try it as a game. Then when you have more confidence, try this method as a 30-minute icebreaker at an otherwise dull meeting to plot the future of something. You can access additional practitioner guidelines by visiting **http://www.spreid.com/book**

Module 6

Creativity Tool: Working with Concepts and Ideas

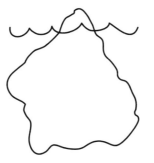

There is a huge difference in the power of an idea and the power of a concept. An idea is just the tip of a much bigger concept – by analogy the mere tip of a far bigger iceberg. A concept is always significantly more influential and much more valuable than a single idea. For example, a pen (idea) is just one aspect of the wider concept of communication. Once identified, a concept can be a very, very powerful springboard to many other new ideas.

What We See

A concept is something often quite vague in description and yet embraces a wide range of individually useful ideas. An idea is often specific and tangible. Once you have created or identified a really good idea it is therefore productive to tunnel back to the parent concept to uncover an even wider range of choices. In my creativity consulting, I have developed and refined a method that is quite easy to apply. It involves unpacking a whole series of concepts that underpin different types of business or situations.

What to Do

This is a 'creative breakers yard' process. We break things down to pieces and reconstitute what we find in a new way. Break a concept or series of concepts from one area of your life or work into component parts. Look at the descriptions of the component elements.

Which of the individual smallest elements that you have unpicked from the concept could become new concepts in their own right? Choose your favourite(s). Just a few words will most probably act as initial triggers. Work up new concepts based on the elements that struck you as most interesting.

TIP

- One insight this method produces is a realisation that the components of great ideas are all around us. The elements are in existence, they just need to be brought together.

Uses

To produce 'break-outs or breakthroughs' from dull or stuck positions. Use where people think things cannot be changed or improved or where innovation is thought to be unlikely.

Further Reading

Additional practitioner guidelines are available at **http://www.spreid.com/book**

Module 7

Creativity Tool: Working with Analogy

'Sometimes we cannot see the wood for the trees.' 'A picture is worth a thousand words.' 'My car goes like a rocket.' 'All is well in the garden.' We use analogies as figures of speech, to quickly convey meaning. We can use the same approach to boost our mental productivity. When we are challenged by something difficult and closely personal it can be easier to solve an analogous problem that is more fun to deal with. In other words, using a playful analogy can help us side-step reality long enough to develop alternative – and importantly, transferable solutions.

What We See

Complex problems often occupy some sort of cluster or family. Some families possess similarities. If you see a solution in one, it may travel across, with a little adaptation, from one family of problems to another. On a practical note, it is always a lot easier to address someone else's problems because we are not wedded to them; we are free to think widely. We use this principle here.

What to Do

Find the heart of the matter. What is your issue centred upon? Look for analogous situations or create an analogy that contains a similar set of characteristics to your own issue. Depart from your own problem and solve the analogous situation, then see what lessons can be used or adapted for your own issue. For example, if you need to acquire some money but the bank manager/source is being uncooperative, consider solving the problem in an abstract way. You could try to figure out, 'How to get blood out of a stone?' Then see if there are any lessons or adaptable ideas.

TIPS

- Take a wider interest in solving problems.
- Everyday obvious examples travel well – good parenting principles, good gardening, public figures – the newspapers are full of examples that may provide useful analogies.

Uses

This is, for me, the best all-round thinking tool. If you can appreciate analogies you will begin to see life's myriad interconnections. There are some initial difficulties involved in using analogies, but once mastered this particular tool is great fun and can generate useful insights in many different work and home-life situations. A skill in using analogy helps us come closer into contact with our intuition.

More information and practitioner guidelines are available at **http://www.spreid. com/book**

Module 8

Mind Mapping *(Tony Buzan)*

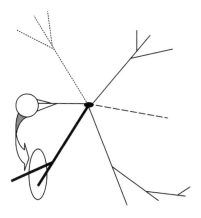

Messy thinking can be more productive than the neat and tidy way. Why? Because our minds are composed of a distributed intelligence. Also, our individual minds store packets of related information and each packet may contain between five and nine items. When we try to think like teacher wants us to, in a linear, neat and tidy way, the information retrieval system in our heads appears to open one packet at a time. The result is that we don't use our minds the way they work naturally. In other words, we get sub-optimal performance because of the linear sequential 'order' we enforce. Using a Mind Map undoes this limitation and can increase our performance.

What We See

This excellent method starts with the notion that 'messiness is OK'. It also allows us to open lots of information packets at once. 'Messiness' stimulates more associations and the release of yet more information and ideas from our mind. Appreciating the value of Mind Mapping by actually using it on something you need to do is the best way forward. Consider planning something, such as a trip or a holiday, using a Mind Map.

A Mind Map captures more meaning than a conventional linear list. The map shows the various strands of reasoning and how different subjects relate to one another.

When used as an aide-mémoire to a presentation, a Mind Map provides a clear view of the structure of the information. This means that during a presentation you are better equipped to take interruptions and can deviate from the main story and quickly recover your position. Having the map helps you express a clear overall view, too. You can demonstrate a well-rounded view of the subject.

What to Do

In an exercise involving this tool take 5 or 10 minutes to map out your thoughts on a piece of A5 card or paper (fold an A4 sheet in half). Or if you are working in a group, use a large flip chart, give everyone a pen and allow anyone to write at will, without explanation.

Begin not at the top, but instead in the middle of a clean unlined page. Represent what occurs to you in a spider diagram as illustrated above. In other words, each leg branching out from the middle represents a group of ideas, people, objects, things to do, etc.

As you write or draw, new material will surface in your mind. In essence, allow your thoughts to flow in an unfiltered way. This is a great way of facilitating a rapid flushing of relevant ideas from your mind. Place the new information released where you think it fits best. Do not worry if the information sits in the 'wrong' place on your map because you can always tidy it up later! The key is to get as much information out of your head and onto paper as quickly as possible.

Some people colour code the different legs of the map to represent different strands of thought. You might also notice or draw in associations and links within your map.

Sample Exercise

You can try this for yourself or with a group. If working with a group, remind them that Tony Buzan originated this particular technique and the term 'Mind Mapping'. His extensive publications on getting more out of our minds are recommended reading.

Use the directions suggested above to map your needs and plans for going on holiday. Put 'holiday' in the middle of the page and see what you generate. You will notice you get more issues, ideas and needs on the table in a shorter space of time than by a conventional linear listing approach.

Why This Is Important

As a divergent thinking tool, Mind Mapping works very well in support of a variety of creative thinking tools. Mind Mapping is a marvellous tool for getting a lot of information down on paper as fast as possible.

TIPS

- You can create a Mind Map first, then tidy it up into a more conventional linear written form later.
- If you are doing an impromptu presentation, keep your small Mind Map in your hand whilst you are presenting. Folded in half, an A5 map fits neatly into a pocket.
- Try to encourage colleagues to use Mind Maps in their work.

Uses

In preparing for and as an aide-mémoire to a presentation. To quickly develop an impromptu speech. To map out complex or data rich subjects.

Overuse

Remember your own Mind Maps will be powerful to you. They may make perfect sense to you but are less likely to mean as much to other people. At some stage, you will need to tidy up the notes and present your thoughts in the commonly understood, linear fashion.

Next Steps

Try Mind Mapping in real situations at home or at work, initially in low-risk settings.

Module 9

Using Generalisation: An Open Thinking Tool

Some of us are afraid to use a generalisation. This is an unnecessary constraint on thinking and self-expression. Generalisations, when used well, can help people to quickly orientate themselves within a wide span of information. Using a generalisation to guide thinking is analogous to saying, 'I don't know exactly which road to take, but I do know we need to be heading north, so let's go north.'

What We See

As with any tool, poor use leads to poor results. A generalisation is a blunt instrument and therefore needs careful handling. Use of generalisations cannot serve a purpose if your audience is inflexible or adopts a narrow, rigid position. A rigid refusal to deal with or use clear generalisations is an unreasonable limitation on free thinking.

We must remain mindful of three inherent limitations when using generalisations:

- A generalisation is an approximate indicator at best.
- A generalisation implies a good degree of elasticity as far as accuracy goes.
- Generalisations only indicate a partial truth.

What to Do

If you choose to generalise it helps if you first make it clear that what you are about to say may be only partially true, and that there will, of course, be clear exceptions to your generalisation. Possibly admit that you know people who are clear exceptions, but then re-assert the general principle as it applies to 'a good number of people/situations/etc.' Be clear that the reason for employing a generalisation is to indicate a direction or a trend and NOT an absolute truth. By taking a careful route around the subject, you may demonstrate a well-rounded appreciation of the issue you are discussing. Fear of looking foolish or rigid adherence to a narrow view of reality can stop people engaging a generalisation.

The General and the Particular

On a practical note, make sure any transitions in reasoning from the general to the particular are well thought through. You should be careful NOT to flip your reasoning between the general and the particular. The way information is dealt with and placed in context is very different in each.

Some of the potential pitfalls of moving our reasoning and conclusions between the general and the particular are illustrated in the following totally fictitious example.

I was once tricked out of some money by a small bald man during a holiday in Prague. That was a specific event, an experience that was 'particular' to me. It is not safe to take this 'particular' experience and turn it into a general rule. Clearly it would be wrong to say, 'All bald men are tricksters,' or 'Small men in Prague cannot be trusted.' However, I might choose to generalise that, 'One should be careful in Prague,' if I had also learned that several other people had experienced a similar misfortune.

To come right out with a generalisation without caveats will not serve you well. A poorly used generalisation would indicate weak thinking.

Why This Is Important

There are realms of thinking in which structured logic works best and others where more elastic thinking is needed. A generalisation is a useful tool that should be allowed occasionally. If people deny you the use of a generalisation, then perhaps the ground has not been prepared or there is a fundamental objection to a broad part of the content of what you are representing. Occasionally the problem is the listener(s) taking a rigid view.

TIPS

- Be careful and circumspect when using generalisations.
- Do not mix the general with the particular.

Uses

Judicious use of an occasional generalisation can help you cover a lot of ground at speed as long as everyone appreciates the limitations. Observation of people who overuse this tool and of those who will not tolerate any generalisations in some areas can be informative.

Overuse

You risk being dismissed for a variety of reasons. You may look a careless fool.

Next Steps

Try to identify people who seem to use generalisations well. Observe what they do. Look for the subtleties and compare their behaviour to someone who does not have the same ability.

Further Reading

Research Aristotle's philosophy of human virtues, in particular his theory of the 'Golden Mean', a mid-point between two vices: two extremes of either excess or deficiency. For example, Aristotle said the virtue of courage was a mid-point between the two vices of cowardice and rashness. Aristotle's idea, as a broad generalisation, works for some, but not all, virtues.

Upgrade Your Models and Tools: Logic
Working on Convergent Focused Thinking

Module 10

Get Your Ducks in a Row

One of the most powerful aspects of logic is the prioritising and sequencing of clearly connected information. Logic assumes that there are clear causes and clear effects, and that one issue is linked in a highly predictable way to the other. Also, it assumes that what you discover in logic is reproducible by other individuals in other places at different times. For example, in logic, one plus one is always equal to two.

Skill in using logic involves understanding the rules that logic and logical people follow. Logical people adopt conventions as well. For example, we agree the names for colours, objects and experiences and embed them in language. To some extent, some behaviours and practices have become so routine they are regarded as 'logical'.

What We See

Developing smart mental skills involves the ability to use a range of intellectual, emotional and social skills; however, in this section we will indulge logic. People who live in a logical world make progress if they develop a logical set of skills combined with sufficient social skills to communicate effectively what they are thinking. People who are seen to be able to quickly go 'directly to the heart of the matter' are particularly valued. People with these quick incisive thinking skills help us to see 'sense'. They are able to filter and distil a lot of information into that which is clear and useful.

Credible Logic

We should remember that perception is reality. When we attempt to communicate with other people, several basic judgements are taken in the first few seconds.

People first ask themselves:

- Should I listen?
- Do I trust you?
- Is this person credible?

If people say 'No' to any of these questions, anything you try to do after that will most likely come to nothing. Your logic will be dismissed before you get a chance to share it. Possession of clear logic is not enough – you must have sufficient personal credibility and social skills to clearly communicate your reasoning and analysis.

What to Do

Logic is to a large extent about discipline, rigour, and clear reproducible sequencing. A neat and tidy way of thinking and 'being' helps. The power of logic demands that another person following your path can reproduce your logical deductions. Logic requires that people build up solid structures of reasoning, often backed up by lots of detail. Ever heard the expression, 'The devil is in the detail'? In many efficient organisations that is true. They, (whoever **they** happen to be) will give you hell if you miss the detail.

The following are ten tips as a guide to the prevailing rules of logic in commercial situations.

- You must have personal credibility. People have a tendency to judge the source before they judge the logic.
- You should have possession of visible, tidy volumes of available information resources AND of a clear, concise, context-relevant précis.
- Your reasoning should have verifiable and generally acceptable foundations. Buttress these foundations using valid precedents.
- Your reasoning should follow a path that is easy to follow and easy to retrace. Make sure your evidence follows a clear sequence and is not overburdened with non-essential detail.
- You should demonstrate appreciation of detail, of the wider contexts and of the boundaries where some of the reasoning might be weak. You should be able to demonstrate an understanding of different rules and common practices.
- You should be concise in what you say – get to the point, politely. Concise, sequential reasoning shows intelligence AND demonstrates that you've spent time figuring out both the big and the detailed picture.
- If there are emotional considerations involved, you should have given these due weight.
- You should demonstrate how things are connected in a way that has relevance and that others will understand.

- When your logic moves to future projection, you should make this transition clear. Any future projections should show a range of risk and possible opportunity. Because the future is open to debate, you may be called upon to defend your case and to demonstrate some flexibility. If you only present the positives you will look naive.
- You should reassert and build trust in who you are and your reasoning ability. Credibility is a form of intellectual credit to be banked.

Logical and Creative People Can and Do Clash

Logical, sequential, consistent reasoning is easy to develop and follow for many people; however, there can be a problem when creative people need to work with more logical people. Often really creative people bounce around from one idea to another but can have great difficulty with focus and ordered sequencing. If you are a creative thinker, try to remember 'the suits' do need a well-ordered, concise presentation that follows a logical route to a logical conclusion, supported by facts and figures. Don't frighten them and don't overwhelm them. Be selective and make sure that what you offer is relatively complete.

> Often 'the suits' hold the purse strings; therefore' don't let yourself down.
> Be smart and 'get your ducks in a row'!

For more information on sequencing, log on to the web site **http://www.spreid. com/book**

The Logic of 'Doing the Obvious'

Effective logic doesn't have to be sophisticated. Take a look at the heads of big organisations. In my experience, quite a number of people in senior management roles are not subtle people. In some success stories, no imagination is required at all – the formula being to get a simple plan and work it, then work it some more. Sometimes repeating an earlier success pattern but on a grander scale can be as effective as a brand new plan. It has the advantage of simplicity, and it is well known to your wider network of supports and employees.

Solutions do not always have to be elegant, creative, well-engineered or researched to death. Quick and dirty, 'first off the blocks' and moving with momentum can create advantages.

Why This Is Important

Logic is the bedrock of Western reasoning. Even if a person chooses to be creative she will still have to employ clear logic in order to communicate with more people to carry out her ideas.

> **TIPS**
>
> - Sometimes it is smart not to try to be too clever with what you are doing. Simplicity has very big advantages when it comes to communicating what needs to be done. Remember to KISS: 'keep it simple, stupid'.
> - Consider what the low-cost, low-tech, less-than-perfect options are before you get too technical.

Uses

Logic and ordered reasoning are the basis for most forms of communicating in business and some parts of emotionally important relationships.

Overuse

Too much use of logic could make a person seem cold and detached, and lacking in imagination. A great cake is made from more ingredients than just flour and water. The taste and pleasure of a well-prepared dish come from the trace ingredients such as spices or flavourings. By analogy, we cannot rely on just the 'bulk ingredient' skills of logic. Conversations and decision-making benefit from human warmth, emotion and humour. Again it is a question of balance. Logic should be graced with appropriate humour.

Module 11

Sense-making and the Logic Cross

Our minds hold information **relative to** other information. The way we build up a sense of meaning in our minds is through these relative associations of different bits of information. We 'scale' what we know.

For example, 'I am taller than her but I am smaller than an elephant.' Our concept of 'height' is a relative one. This sort of relative reasoning can be understood by someone else. Sailors, pilots or anyone trying to find their way across wide-open featureless seas have used **relative** maps for centuries. When we look for a place on a map, we use grid references. Two points crossed over tell us where we are, relative to other places. An individual piece of information can be difficult to place if it is not relative to something else. Using knowledge in **a relative way** helps us to learn and to explore our sense of what is logical. Knowing that our minds create meaning by linking different bits of information in a relative way, we can take two bits of information and generate a new set of insights. We can find our way within a sea of facts. Crossing two sets of information allows us to create four relationships within a grid. This simple process can help us to think about information in some sort of **relevant context**.

What We See

When we are faced with a lot of complex information, this particular tool allows us to begin to search out relatively logical or meaningful relationships. Mapping information in a relative way is so useful that this method has become a favourite of management consultants and business school academics. They use this pattern to deduce meaning and to provide insights into complex situations.

One of the simplest ways of creating a sense of meaning when faced with foggy or nebulous information is to try to hold it in relationship to something else. We employ the trick of thinking in relative terms in our thinking about other people as much as we do in our **thinking about work problems**. Person/option A is better than B and C is better than A. We judge things in a relative way.

What to Do

Consider the important forces at work. Start by crossing two factors to see what sort of relative meanings are created. Crossing two sets of information creates a four-square grid. This simple 'logic cross' produces four spaces, each of which can be more clearly defined by their extremes.

When you construct a grid, often each axis may show a scale with 'high' at one end and 'low' at the other. The important first step is to distil out the major forces at work and then spend a little time crossing a variety of options to see if a useful sense-making pattern emerges.

For example:

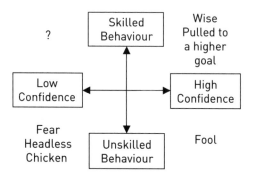

Above is an example using a scale of attitudes involving a confidence scale with the extent to which some one could be described as 'skilled.' How would you describe the fourth person in the top-left quadrant?

The meanings within these four quadrants cannot be absolute, because each one is formed from two variable elements. Therefore, when we create a sense of something we accept the use of approximations. Our reasoning here is not absolute, but is all the richer for it.

Uses

- Crossing interesting information helps us make sense of our reality.
- Contrasting different high-impact uncertainties is one of the central techniques of 'scenario planning'.

Overuse

Sometimes crossing over different concepts or forces produces nothing of value.

Module 12

Sense-making – Nine Space Grid

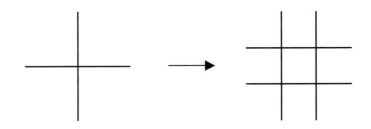

Sometimes a four-square sense-making grid is too crude and something richer is needed. A nine-square grid can provide more detail and better insights and may guide us toward better decisions. For a demonstration, see the example, 'Can't Pay – Won't Pay' below.

What We See

A richer set of information can be deduced when a nine-square grid, instead of a four-square grid, overlays two interacting sets of information.

Exercise

Create a four-square grid first. Use the axis of 'ability to pay' with another axis, 'willingness to pay'. How would you categorise the various types of debtor, and what would be your policy toward each type of person? Would you change your billing policy as a result of viewing matters in this way? Your four-part grid would be as below, but would probably not create a sufficiently rich picture to help you develop a reasonable decision-making policy.

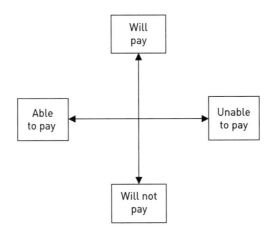

Now try populating a nine-part grid in our model for 'debtors'. Then using this same grid, review what your decisions might be according to the level of necessity of a service. Consider two situations: what would your policy for debt recovery be when the product was: (a) a non-essential service or (b) a life-essential service.

A nine-part chart might look like this:

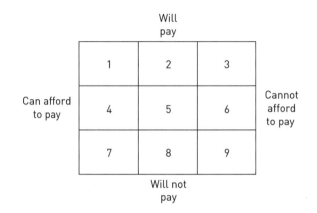

First segment the people you deal with into the categories above. If the service is non-essential, then denial of access or court action to cover losses may be appropriate. It is probably pointless and simply punitive to chase 9 to recover payment. It's probably easier to chase 4 and then 7. But what if the product or service is vital to human life, such as water or warmth? Regarding the supply of such an essential product, how will you proceed in regard to the different types of customer? This model makes one large assumption that would have to be tested: namely, can you populate your customer database with enough tangible evidence to profile individuals in a reasonable and accurate way? Assuming you can collect the information you need, you may begin to ask some important questions. This nine-part chart is richer because it can guide you to ask less obvious questions, such as: If we take action to support 9, what do we then do about 3 or 6? Furthermore, how will we differentiate between 2 and 3?

Clearly some people in this model of reality are building up debts to stay alive, whilst others are confronting the charges for different reasons. If the imbalance becomes a moral question, then the impact of the imbalances will eventually come home to hurt the owners of the debt in the form of bad press, political unrest or enforced change.

The decision matrix shown in the example above gets even cloudier when you map a service such as 'essential health-care'. From an individual perspective, health-care is always vital, but if the state is paying, or is seen as totally responsible, then in reality the state will ultimately be forced to ration services in areas it deems to be essential, which may or may not include you. The cost of maintaining life can be open-ended; however, governments have finite budgets. Ultimately, someone somewhere has to take some very difficult decisions, and then sleep with a clear conscience of having done the best she can, given the open-ended nature of the problem. A model such as this can help partition the decision spaces.

What to Do

Decide what your intersecting lines of reasoning are and then produce nine spaces using the grid illustrated above. The definition of types or a segmentation of meanings becomes easier with nine spaces to play with. This particular modelling process works when you are dealing with well-defined logic. Each space has some meaning and relevance and can guide your thinking. Work through the exercise below.

TIPS

- Examine each space. Which spaces seem to offer the most interesting contradictions or questions?
- Consider how you will validate each category in a reasonable way and what would cause you to reclassify something or someone. Who or what rules will be used to arbitrate?
- Before you take any decisions, consider how you will manage the different categories and remain 'fair'.

Uses

Many and varied, where a richer picture is required – perhaps signalled by a sense of irritation that a four-square grid is just too simple.

Module 13

Sense-making – A Variable Grid

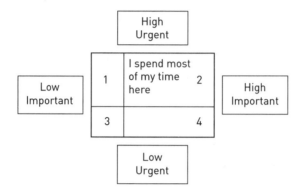

Few things in life fall into neat equal boxes. In fact, we all have some sort of bias operating in our lives. We can more accurately map what is happening and take bias into account by allowing the cross-hairs on a four-square grid to move, as in the 'use of time' example illustrated above. Some things get emphasised at the expense of others – that is the essence of a bias. This pattern helps us to look at the total picture, and the merits and demerits of individual trade-offs between different priorities, issues or resources.

What We See

In this model the lines are not fixed and can move to reflect a shift of emphasis and changing priorities. Using the illustrated example above, we can see how one individual uses his time at work. Different people will have different patterns according to how they choose to use their total time available. This particular model can help us to interpret our preferences as part of a whole pattern, taking bias into account.

What to Do

As in the previous model, consider the major forces at work in a situation. Then work out what percentage of the issue you are studying belongs in each of the four sections, and move the cross-hairs to reflect this.

Uses

Many and varied – where a more rounded view is desired. Once you have identified the major forces at work, this sort of tool can help you consider where the emphasis is placed and what sacrifices might be required if you choose a different pattern.

Tuning the Controls

Module 14

Two Major Directions for Thinking

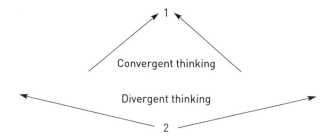

Our thoughts and reason tend to follow one of the two major pathways illustrated above. People often adopt a preference for one style as their major thinking skill, which is reinforced in some way; for example, their preferred pattern is enjoyable or gets results. Limiting our mental faculties to just one pattern means we limit our potential; smart people are proficient in both. The first thinking path (1) involves focus: getting things done, whilst the second (2) involves the opposite: an open-ended diverging pattern where discovery and looking around are important. Each style or pattern has its particular benefits and shortcomings.

> *Our preferred thinking pattern is generally reflected in shopping behaviour. Men and women – generally – will shop in a particular way, depending on the product.*
>
> *Retailers have worked this out and have arranged their stores accordingly. Focused, mission shopping = neat, tidy clear lines of sight, clarity of offer, not too much distraction. Exploration shopping involves discovery, browsing, lots of choice, variety and crowded racks.*

What We See

Whilst single-minded, focused thinking may work well in some circumstances, this may actually limit us in other important areas of life. To illustrate, imagine yourself as a fighting crab. The type of crab that has one truly huge claw! Imagine how the crab moves and how it carries itself. Our crab cannot do anything but lead with its one huge claw. You may find it difficult to picture where the other smaller claw is or to imagine how such an undeveloped little claw can ever be of any use.

Now imagine a human brain equally lopsided. Intellectually, our development tends to produce minds and behaviours that are about as lopsided as the distribution of the crab's fighting muscle. In survival terms, one huge claw beats two average ones in a fight every time, but what if the fighting stops and new rules are applied? What once provided an advantage becomes a serious evolutionary liability.

The Two Basic Thinking Pathways

1. Convergent Thinking (Focus)

Thinking focused on quick results = convergent focused thinking. This type of thinking quickly narrows down to a closed clear decision. This is the basis of simple logic. Convergent thinking is used by warriors, purposeful hunters of things and information, active decision-makers – anyone who is in control or who likes to take action. It can often be used in an assertive, directive way, as a sort of aggressive, 'hunting' logic. Consider how the reasoning used in debates and in courts is based on an adversarial pattern. People who use this particular style exclusively can sometimes think and behave in narrow, over-directed ways: 'bulls in china shops'.

Why a Focused Thinking Skill Is Important

Focused thinking is great for getting a quick result – if one is available.

It is an essential pattern if something is to happen. Thinking this way is often specific, clear and defined, and as a result, people can align with this way of thinking.

but

A lot of people can be lined up efficiently behind the wrong idea or process.

2. Divergent Thinking (Open-ended Exploration)

Playful, creative, **divergent** thinking people who primarily use this path may be viewed as vague or dippy in their thinking and may be incapable of taking or concluding important decisions or actions.

The mental disciplines and rules for **creative (divergent)** thinking are the opposite of **focused (convergent)** thinking. Clearly there is scope for a clash or significant misunderstanding when people fail to understand which pattern of thinking preferences is being exercised.

Why an Exploratory Thinking Skill Is Important

Creative, divergent thinking is great for exploration and looking around.

It is an essential creative thinking process. If you need to be considerate, divergent, open-minded thinking can help you get a wider perspective.

but

For a variety of reasons people who predominantly prefer this pattern can find it difficult to align with each other. Getting people with imagination to work together is a lot like 'trying to herd cats'. Different management styles are needed here.

What to Do

When you meet other people, be mindful of the direction your own AND their thoughts follow. If your aim is to cover a lot of ground in depth, but quickly, then attempt to get people's minds to line up with one particular pattern at a time. Be clear about the direction and shape of the thinking required. Having an awareness of the direction of the thinking paths in operation by you and others can help you make progress.

If you want focused answers, ask focused questions. If you want an exploratory, open response, than phrase the questions in an open way. Be aware of the rules and the usual outcomes of each pattern.

If you want results according to the manual, ask someone who demonstrates clear, focused abilities. But if you need something imaginative and you have the time, use someone who prefers divergent thinking. In the second case, the answers may be incomplete, late or quite different from what you expected.

If you know your own thinking is messy, then apply discipline. Encourage yourself to follow both paths when you need to think something all the way through to a productive conclusion.

The more we practise new skills the better we are likely to be.

TIPS

- Keep it simple if you can: creative divergent thinking is disruptive, takes time, is likely to be messy and may not always produce a result in the time you specify.
- Make a conscious choice of the direction you want the thinking to follow, and then channel the process.
- If you believe you are low on creative, divergent thinking see the modules on self-awareness and creativity, or team up with someone who will complement your skills.
- If you believe you are low on the ability to think in a focused, achievement-orientated way, look at the modules on self-awareness and logic, or team up with some one with the skills you lack.
- Practise, practise, practise.

Uses

To better orchestrate your own or others' thoughts in a desired direction. You can mirror the thinking patterns in others and provide the type of help they are expecting. If you are a retailer, you may choose to lay out your premises to suit the prevailing mindset of your customers. Knowing the predominant thinking-path preferences of the people to whom you relate puts you in a better position to influence them.

Overuse

Someone who relies too much on focused thought-processing risks being narrow-minded, lacking in imagination, cold perhaps. Someone who overindulges a divergent world may start many things and finish none of them – perhaps appearing vague and uncommitted. Without clear cause and effect, without boundaries, someone who is locked into divergent thinking may eventually wonder what is the point of anything. (Paradoxically, creativity can be provoked by constraints.)

Next Steps

Observe your own and other people's reasoning patterns and the directions their thoughts and behaviours seem to take.

Last Words

As a high-performance individual, it is not wise to rely heavily on one particular thinking pathway or any particular thinking tool. Great thinking skill is a matter of balance. A genius is distinguished by width, breadth and depth of thought, plus the ability to flex and move quickly between these two major thinking paths.

Further Reading

See the modules on logic and creativity in Territory One, and the module entitled Dreamer/Critic/Realist in Territory Two. These two patterns of thinking also significantly affect how we relate to other people. See module 17.

Module 15

Frames of Reference

We are born as 'blank slates' but we quickly build up a mental safe zone within which we can make easier, quicker judgements based on the knowledge we have collected. As we learn and experience life, we build up our very own personal sets of guidelines, rules, truths, boundaries and beliefs about how to live. We develop personal 'frames of reference'. We each create our own sub-frames; for example, how to dress, how to write, how we conduct ourselves, etc. These many sub-frames add up to one big personal 'true view' of how we see and experience reality. Each person's greater frame of reference is unique because our growth and experiences of reality will be different. Someone who has remained open to a lot of experience will have a rich body of personal experience to call upon.

What We See

When you are experiencing life according to what you have come to expect, you feel safe inside your frame of reference – your reality. When you operate within your frame of reference, the world feels logical, rational, known and predictable. Inside such frames, you can think and decide quickly and efficiently based on what you already know. Your employment and wider social credibility are dependent on the extent to which you fill up and refresh your frames of reference.

A high level of mental efficiency is not available outside your frame of reference. Outside your frame, you may feel unsure, sometimes anxious, sometimes excited. For example, consider how you felt during a 'personal first', such as learning to drive. When one experiences an earth tremor for the first time, frames of reference are thrown into disarray; you feel anxious because reality is not performing as expected. These new experiences are intense, high energy and quite demanding because you are learning. You could not live all your life like this – you'd simply burn out.

Frames therefore help us live harmonious, biologically efficient lives. We learn when we need to or when circumstances demand it.

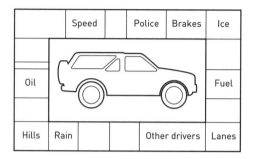

	Speed		Police	Brakes	Ice
Oil					Fuel
Hills	Rain			Other drivers	Lanes

For most of the time, therefore, our minds tend to run on autopilot. Our routines and behaviours are called up from our frames of reference as needed. Doing something familiar, such as driving your car or cooking that favourite dish, is not as demanding as the first attempt was. Your mind is 'free' to think about other things; part of you is switched to automatic. One of several downsides of habitual 'unthinking' routines is that you may do things that were correct at a point in the past, but are strange or wrong now. Also, you may not see a challenge looming, or that big new opportunity you've been hoping for, when it presents itself in a novel way. A fixed frame of reference can be a trap.

What to Do

- Be aware of what the working assumptions are for you and for the people closest to you at home and at work.
- Be alert to differences in working assumptions.
- Often the 'truth' is just a set of working assumptions.
- Assumptions are often 'tacit' or not consciously open to view. They occasionally need to be made explicit.
- Deeply held assumptions may be tagged to very strong emotions. Approach these diligently.
- Assumptions can be addressed logically or creatively.
- The most obvious working assumptions are the most difficult to make explicit.
- See the guidelines from creative thinking techniques that play around with assumptions.

Why This Is Important

Frames of reference are a basic biological necessity. They make us efficient in our work and the rest of our lives. They help us to live harmoniously and to conserve mental energy. We would burn out early in our lives without them.

If we take a close look at our individual and collective frames of reference, we find many aspects are not based soundly on absolute truths. Many of our beliefs and behaviours are instead based upon working assumptions that we believe to be valid. The validity and assumptions of what is actually true can be changed. Take 'money', for example. Money is not actually worth anything in itself. Money only works because we all agree rates of exchange for bits of paper that at one time were underpinned by hoards of gold in government vaults. Western governments no longer keep gold as currency collateral.

TIPS

- Be sensitive to situations in which people may have an investment in holding onto what you or others may regard as outdated or invalid assumptions.
- Changing assumptions involves changing a sense of reality.
- Attempts to change deeply held assumptions can be advantageous and/or dangerous.
- People (communities and systems) have quite different working assumptions regarding their patterns and tolerances. (See later module concerning certainty.)
- An individual or a collective frame of reference can be a trap.

Uses

If you wish to be innovative you need to understand collective assumptions. Good for creating and dealing with change. An awareness of other people's working assumptions can help you predict how they might see reality and how they may behave or react.

Next Steps

If you wish to change something, think about what assumptions make the thing 'true', then test them. Think just as much about your own assumptions as those that other people may be operating under. If an opportunity arises to discuss working assumptions regarding other people be well prepared and tread very carefully.

Decisions

Module 16

Basic Clear-cut Decision-making

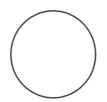

The world simply 'is'.

Simple situations often only require simple decisions. The simplest decision is an absolute one. We choose one side of two opposites, such as either yes or no, right or wrong, this or that, plus or minus.

For example, two plus two is always four. Any other answer is wrong. The process is clear, reproducible and beyond doubt. This is a binary decision process and it works best within well-bounded, highly defined and regulated environments.

What We See

Choices in this well-defined area of reality can be made using the clearest, most efficient forms of logic. This binary, either/or structure of decision-making is a form of linear logic that lies at the heart of a lot of fundamental computing software. Today these simple, repetitive decisions can be and are being automated by machines, with less and less human intervention.

In a state of pure innocence there are no choices.

A Visual Model

The first illustration in this module, the empty circle, represents a world of information. There is no right and there is no wrong. The world simply 'is'. For the sake of this illustration, let's say that everything within conscious awareness lies within the circle. There has been no differentiation between things and all thoughts are without judgement or place or time. There is no relativity and therefore no meaning.

When we choose to make a decision, we attempt to classify good and bad or right and wrong information, or we try to separate useful from not useful. We try to create meaning by 'comparison'. This reasoning is represented below.

Information is judged.

The information falls into clearly
defined, absolute areas.

A cleanly divided circle represents the simplest kind of problem in which clear-cut results can be achieved. If we apply clear judgement, we look for a clear line between what is correct and what is incorrect. Information is then judged in a relative way. In this case, we can make a clear cut between what is right and what is wrong. An example of a 'clear-cut' problem would be a request to find the fastest way to travel between two fixed points; for example, from your hometown to the capital city. More time and study will lead to a better quality answer, until a perfect route is found. More study = a better result is an assumption that works very well with this sort of decision.

In this case, a clear answer is possible and is obvious once the work has been done. One hundred percent of the correct information falls on one side of the divide. Here we have complete certainty; we know the decision to be a clear on/off or right/wrong one.

This particular sort of decision can be maximised; 100% efficiency can be achieved. One might refer to this type of problem as being 'maximal' or 'clear-cut'. Regrettably, naive managers sometimes assume all problems are like this and that their role is to solve all problems. They create unnecessary anxiety by driving other people to come up with clear-cut, detailed answers in situations where this particular simple process does not work. Attempts to find the right answer result in what I call the search for the 'spreadsheet for everything'.

What to Do

Understand the requirements of logic. Realise that not all decisions are complex. Make decisions quickly when the decision is a simple one, and move on to the next issue.

Filters and Hurdles

If your decision issue involves simple material, but with perhaps lots of detail or several equally logical choices, then it can be helpful to begin by agreeing what factors will distinguish a good choice from an inferior one *before you start processing*. This sort of decision-making lends itself to simple spreadsheet logic. Record the choices along the top, place one judgement factor per horizontal row, then score off each one leaving a total at the bottom line. Highest (or sometimes lowest) score wins.

Some people describe these decision hurdles as 'filters'. If the problems consistently resist a clear answer, then you may be dealing with a higher level of problem, involving ambiguous issues.

Why This Is Important

If you do not understand that different classes of problems require different solution strategies, you will quickly be out of your depth in a complex, dynamic or competitive environment.

TIPS

- Have more than one decision-making skill in your mental tool bag.
- Be prepared to use more than one problem-solving strategy.

Uses

This level of decision-making is used in computer programming and relatively straightforward right/wrong type decision-making. If most of your job involves this kind of repetitive decision-making, then start to look for something higher up the food chain before the job gets taken over by a machine.

Overuse

In such highly defined and bounded stable environments, simple logic can become ritualistic. When the facility to think is not called upon, we are at risk. Where people have lived for a long time in such simple environments, they may be misled in assuming that all decisions are possible using logic, a routine or a ritual procedure. When faced with the real world of complex problems they cannot cope. For the moment though, we will focus on simple decisions.

Module 17

Two Very Different Problem-solving Patterns

She Wants to Look Arround
But
He Wants to Give a Solution

In problem solving, there are two clearly opposed patterns. These two mental processing patterns are not explicit, they are hidden, but they do have a big impact on how we think and behave. One involves a strong preference for looking around first, whilst the other seeks to focus and close down a problem quickly. When two people using opposing thinking patterns attempt to solve a problem they generate frustration because the 'rules' for one pattern contradict the rules of the other. The resulting 'shape' of their dialogue, would, if we drew it, look like the crude 'Christmas tree' sketch above. One person in turn attempts to diverge/open up the conversation and go looking around, whilst the other attempts to converge and close down with answers.

> **EXAMPLE**
>
> The way we think is also reflected in the way we behave. Take, for example, the experience of two quite different people going shopping together. One person might wish to be mission-headed, get a result quite quickly and then go home to do something more interesting, whilst his partner may want to spend much more time looking around before **actually** parting with money and buying something. Expectations, thinking and behaviour are all now mismatched; the minimum outcome is frustration, resignation or perhaps an argument.

What We See

Below I've described, in very crude terms, how the two patterns might look from the point of view of an onlooker observing someone helping someone else to deal with a problem. Christmas-tree thinking shows us how not to mix type one with type two problem solving. Their sequence of processing is as follows:

Type One (The Closer) – Convergent Pattern

This is a quick closing process.

1 Hear the problem.
2 Suggest a small number of things the problem owner should do. There is an imperative to 'act now'.
3 Close the discussion, move on to something new.

Type Two (The Explorer) – Mostly a Divergent Pattern

This is the *opposite* of type one. The divergent pattern is about wide scanning, looking around and turning over all the stones to see what is there. Only with full knowledge of the whole territory will the problem owner then reflect and consider making a decision based on choices.

1 Hear the problem.
2 Ask open questions (do not make suggestions).
3 Owner encouraged to look around widely, and encouraged to consider whether anything has been missed.
4 Considerations of wider picture including feelings, other people, situations and material issues.
5 When she has had sufficient opportunity to look around, (i.e., divergent/open thinking) the problem owner signals what she believes the choices are.
6 If satisfied, the problem owner will then reflect and possibly test out the preferred choices. If not satisfied, she may continue to look around.
7 Then she may make a choice.

As a very broad brush *generalisation* women are often comfortable switching between convergent focus and open divergent thinking. Men, generally speaking are not nearly as reflective and often show quite a strong preference for focus and are generally less familiar or comfortable with the open divergent thinking patter

When our minds pull in opposite directions, it is easy to set up a misunderstanding. You will see a breakdown in communication in these examples because neither person is aware of the direction in which the other intuitively wants to travel in thought and action.

EXAMPLE

When two friends with the opposite problem-solving preferences meet, we see a Christmas-tree pattern developing. Type two, 'the explorer', indicates the nature of the problem but type one, 'the closer', keeps offering closing down solutions ('Why don't you do this..?'), when his 'explorer' friend really wants to 'look around'. The conversation ends with a sense of frustration for both.

Now let's consider the two people acting out the same situation but in the opposite direction. Type two, 'the explorer' is trying to help type one, 'the closer'. 'The explorer' wants to help but then seems unable to provide clear solutions. From the point of view of 'the closer', his friend seems to be avoiding the central issue and waffling, when all that 'the closer' wants is wants a couple of quick, 'Do this and you will get a result' suggestions.

What to Do

Be aware of the directions thoughts can travel in and the rules governing each pathway. Watch out for the pattern employed by the other person, and try mirroring it in a constructive way. For example, you could try explaining what you believe the other person's thinking process is, asking if your interpretation is correct and then suggesting the next direction.

Why This Is Important

When we understand the direction of thought and the sequence in which we process things, we can communicate in a much more productive and influential way.

TIP

- Remember these patterns are preferences, not rigid behaviour patterns. We all possess, to differing degrees, abilities in both.

Uses

Improved, clear communication and more productive discussions. Good influencing. Steering a creative discussion, negotiating, conflict resolution and strategic thought process.

Next Steps

Observe other people's patterns in arguments, discussions and problem-solving. Choose to go shopping with people who are likely to follow your pattern and set free those who are not.

Be considerate of people who dislike your preferred pattern. When you need help, take time to consider the shape of the dialogue you want and then guide people who offer help along the thinking path you require.

Feeling and Thinking

Module 18

Productive Use of Tension

The ability to tolerate awkward feelings regarding what we do not yet know is, after self-awareness, one of the most important aspects of our minds, which allows us to break out and upgrade to a higher level of thinking. If you are self-aware but cannot tolerate the uncertainties you discover, then progress will falter. Developing your creative thinking ability will help build up such tolerance.

Building up a level of tolerance requires a high degree of openness and a willingness to mentally 'travel without judgement'. The initial outward journey during a creative exercise – away from present reality – is pleasant and amusing, as this is the playful stage. By contrast, the return journey back toward reality carries an obligation to convert playful thinking into solid ideas. This involves a real sense of tension. During this last phase, people must fight to hold off their critical analytical processes AND at the same time discover practical new ideas. The easy but wrong answer at this last stage is to allow our minds to release the sense of tension by allowing easy, obvious and rational possibilities as completion points. When this happens the very lifeblood of a good idea is quickly turned into banality by rational thought.

Learning to accept this awkward and sometimes quite irritating feeling of tension is a necessary step in developing creative thinking ability. Tension must be held and harnessed and not released until very good ideas are driven out from under its cloud.

We will see how important it is to develop a tolerance of feelings of tension when we look at higher levels of mental ability in the later sections of this book.

Module 19

Escaping the Frame

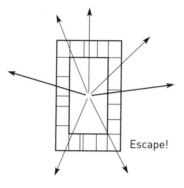

Escape!

A significant breakthrough in upgrading your thinking is the ability to employ both major thinking pathways. Proficiency involves maximising how well and how fast you think inside your frame of reference (logic) AND your ability to escape the confines of what you assume to be true through divergent creative thinking. The above model illustrates this. In simple terms, 'divergent' open thinking allows us to cross the boundaries of our frames of reference. Once beyond the relative safety and efficiency of our frames of reference, we are free to think creatively, beyond currently accepted limitations. You should be aware that strong feelings will be engaged when you cross the border of your frame of reference.

What We See

Energy is always involved at the point where a frame boundary is crossed. When we deal at the edge of anyone's sense of reality there is always an emotional reaction. Fortunately, 99.9% of the time in my workshops I see laughter. If people aren't laughing, then the creative techniques are not working properly; there isn't enough permission, freedom or energy. An 'aha!' moment – a moment where a great idea is 'released' – is always charged with energy and strong feelings.

What to Do

The 'escape' model described below is the basic 'vanilla' concept underpinning a range of creative thinking techniques that follow this simple pattern:

1 Describe and park. State the problem/issue to be considered as simply as possible. Then forget it till later.

2 Playtime (divergent open thinking). Use a playful process to take your mind(s) on an unusual journey. Promote laughter. Collect bizarre thoughts that are very distant from the original issue. This step will not work without laughter – so play! Have fun!

3 Tension phase (synthesis). Force fit these bizarre thoughts into the context of the issue to stimulate further unusual ideas. Keep the tension between 'normal and bizarre' open as long as possible.

4 Dig for gems (synthesis). Try to find any powerful concepts underlying the ideas, as these lead to even more fertile ground.

5 Collect and build (moving toward convergent focused thinking). Harvest and reinforce the best of the ideas that come forth.

There are many ways of using this particular pattern. See the creative thinking tools given at the beginning of the book.

When we use our minds in a productive, creative way, both major thinking paths ('open/creative' and 'focused/hunting' thinking) are employed at different times. Groups need to coordinate which pattern is in use in order to be constructive. An ability to use the feelings generated in a positive way is important.

Why This Is Important

If we stay safe within our 'boxed-in frames of reference', we may feel secure for a while, but come the wind of change we will be ill-prepared to evolve and move forward. A safe frame of reference leads to healthy habits but can also become a stagnant trap. It is healthy to challenge our minds, to take the risk or the pleasure in venturing outside to exercise our imaginations and to discover, invent and create new things.

TIPS

- If there is no sense of fun or energy, the process is probably not going to work at this time. Watch for 'flashes' of inspiration later.
- Be self-aware and try not to resort to accepted traditional terminology.
- Be prepared to take risks in what is said.
- Go with the unusual and the bizarre or anything that provokes laughter.
- Try to resist any attempt to diffuse the sense of tension by rushing into obvious but much weaker ideas within 'safe' territory.

Use

This combined model helps us realise another role for our emotions. Our emotions signal we are onto something new and that a learning opportunity (or a threat) is imminent. The model helps us see a sense of direction when we are being creative.

Next Steps

Choose an occasion when you believe the rational route has gone dry and you believe new ideas are required. Then try a creative thinking tool.

Last Words

There are lots of different ways of developing a creative way of thinking. Creative thinking is an essential part of your intellectual skill set. Most people will find it possible to grasp and use at least one of the creative thinking techniques I provided earlier in this section. My most common advice for the few who cannot grasp these methods is to team up with someone with creative mental skills. Then do what *you* are good at.

Module 20

Change, and Broken Frames of Reference

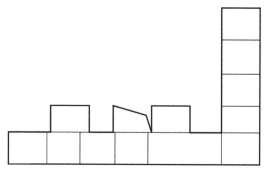

People cope with change in different ways; however, we all have our limits. Aware-ness of these limits and of the pattern of events in our minds during change can help us weather difficult transitions. Frames of reference are mental constructions within which we live more securely. We tend not to function too well with damaged frames of reference. Our personal frames can be broken by changes in relationships, changes in where we live and work, changes in status or new information.

Different people build, reinforce and repair their frames of reference in different ways and at quite different rates. We should therefore handle with care frames that encompass the deepest held beliefs in ourselves and others. This principle applies to individuals AND communities. A lack of consideration here can be cruel to your-self and others. If not handled properly, change can lead to long-lasting wounds and limitations on performance.

What We See

Our individual and community frames of reference are dynamic; learning and new experiences can change them. They can be built up and reinforced as well as damaged and repaired. Often people who are 'in control' will make changes at a pace with which they feel comfortable. The trouble is that often the people who are affected do not have the same feeling of control and may feel much more chal-lenged than the person controlling events. Different people adapt at different speeds.

The Impact of Change – An Example: Falling in Love

By way of illustration as to how important this concept is, recall the first time you fell in love. How did you feel? The experience was overwhelming as you became aware of something quite magical.

Despite very strong feelings of loyalty and affection, quite a lot of people do not sustain this first love relationship. One side or the other decides the relationship is not for them. Now contrast how 'first love' felt with the feelings associated with the end of this first very special relationship. How did you then feel? Often the terms used to describe how people felt at the end are structural; for instance, 'My world fell apart.' The reason for this is that the 'world' in which we were in love was built on an unspoken, deeply held assumption concerning time. We seem to be hard-wired with an assumption that 'love is forever'.

When one person leaves the relationship, but is still physically present, a huge con-tradiction is set up. In divorce, one partner may go as far as to say that the experience would have been easier to deal with if the other one had died. In a way, a separation feels worse because the relationship is dead but the other person is still there.

Staying with the emotional roller coaster, the next interesting question to pose is, 'How soon can you fall in love again if someone you love has left you?' It is not going to happen in a day or so, is it? A new loving relationship cannot be formed overnight. We feel as if all of the pieces are in the wrong place; trust may have been undermined and we may feel empty and unable to give anything to love. Time is required to repair the damaged 'reality'. We need time to rebuild our per-sonal frames of reference. This hard lesson applies to any significant change in our lives. Clearly this demonstrates how people need time to deal properly with change – both at home and at work.

Change and Conflict

Powerful emotional reactions can be created when an important frame of reference is damaged. A 'raw nerve' is touched, a wound is opened and a sense of insecu-rity can be created. Generally, many people dislike change at home or at work and may try to avoid it or rush it through in order to get back to a sense of security. Conflicts inevitably arise. One side or the other may have had a hand directly or indirectly in changing something seen as trivial by one, but which is highly signifi-cant to the other. The grievance may not have been made explicit. In haste to close the 'trivial', a conflict is enraged. Broken frames need care, attention and time.

What to Do

We all endure change during the course of our lives. Try to manage the extent to which you or others are subject to change and take more time to deal with it. We may feel most vulnerable when we feel out of control or when we do not trust others to have our best interests at heart in what we perceive to be 'new, danger-ous situations'. If you can, insist on being involved in planning how change will happen, or at least decide for yourself how you propose to react to change. This will then create some sense of control and lead to lower anxiety.

Why This Is Important

I use the highly personal example of loss in love to anchor the idea that when we attempt to change other people's 'reality', their ability to adapt and repair how they see and interact with the world can take longer than we might imagine. If you are a leader delivering change remember this. New frames of reference take time to build up and rebuild.

TIPS

From personal experience, I know it is best to try to face life's significant challenges one at a time. Serious challenges include moving house, public speaking, a birth or death in the family, change or loss of job, and relationship changes at home. We all have tolerance levels for change but as a general rule I have found that even if you are in peak physical condition:

- One significant life change will rock your boat.
- Two major changes at the same time will serious stretch you.
- Three serious changes at the same time may be endured for only a short time, after which you are at considerable risk.
- Give yourself, and others, time to change and try not to overwhelm people with too many changes at once. If there are a lot of changes to be made, sharing the sense of control can help. Get people involved in the how, when and what of change.
- Deal honestly with your own feelings; let them be expressed. Bottling up feelings leads to a bad form of mental constipation, which will erupt at a later date, possibly beyond your own control.
- Be clear about what assumptions you are changing and what is going to take their place.
- Be clear where the anchors are (see later module).
- People who are in a position of authority directing change that is very negative or hurts relationships will, despite the fact they are in control, need personal help. This is important and should not be overlooked. Leaders and authority figures may feel it necessary to defer any feelings so that they can 'push past' the obstacles and make progress. Buried feelings have a habit of popping up later in unexpected ways. If not managed properly, such deferred feelings can be the root of some serious damage to a leader's mental health, performance, relationships and career.
- Accept that life is neither linear nor straightforward. The willow bends in a storm, whilst the rigid oak may split.
- Find and preserve hope. What has been lost can be found again, most likely within a completely new and probably quite different experience.

Uses

In change and challenge situations. Remember the broken frame idea when facing or leading change. To remind change leaders that their own frames may be changed in a different way and that they too will need special personal support. This model can be useful in dealing with conflicts.

Last Words

Dealing effectively with major change is about many things, but deeply held assumptions and expectations are often at the heart of the matter. Our deepest assumptions need to be examined and if necessary recreated so that we can develop a renewed sense of personal security. At the same time, we need to manage our own and others' expectations, because this is the font from which hope and ambition spring. All of this takes care, attention and time. Any attempt to rush will bruise hope and expectations. Always remember that hope is a precious and quite fragile thing.

Relationships

Module 21

The Way We Frame Relationships

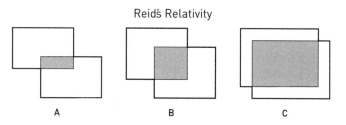
Reid's Relativity

A   B   C

The way we think about our relationships with other people influences the way we behave. We have ideas about our relationships that may or may not be correct NOW. We should remember that between two people there are two completely independent mental maps of the one relationship. People generally don't stop to check the extent to which these maps actually match up. Our assumptions regarding our important relationships could be all wrong.

We can easily misunderstand the quality and depth of our relationships, especially with the passage of time. We may believe that the characteristics of a relationship are as in 'C' but the other person may think of our relationship as illustrated by 'A'

An unrealistic view of the depth and quality of important relationships is likely to lead to unfulfilled expectations, confusion, frustration and reduced performance.

EXAMPLE

As a naive young manager working for the first time in a large corporate office, I discovered that 'friendships' evaporated when I needed support in an ego-laden and important senior management meeting.

I have to say that I'm still learning, albeit slowly. I once had (I believed) a good friendship with a man I had known since we were students. One day, he said, 'Stephen, you know, you only ever seem to telephone me when you need something.'

I replied, 'On reflection, now that you mention it, I'm sorry to say that seems about right.'

'OK,' he said, and with that he put the phone down and I haven't heard from him since. To be honest, I haven't had the nerve to call him back either. I believed our friendship was in C, but it seems I pushed it to A and then right off the scale. Or perhaps it only ever was at A. I'll never know.

What We See

Each person's frame of reference is unique. Whilst we may share differing amounts of common ground, we each of us exhibit different rational and emotional preferences. We can benefit from knowing the true nature of our relationships and the extent to which we have common ground. This varies in perception, in time and in context, so it is wise to understand and refresh who your friends actually are and who your friends were. You may also have overlooked someone extending real friendship overtures. (Self-awareness again.)

What to Do

It is essential to remember that in all relationships over time, the other person's personal frame of reference can and will migrate, sometimes in a different direction from your own. Periodically review your assumptions about your relationships. Consider and seek advice on what is best for the future of the relationship. All things evolve and decay with time. Sometimes it is necessary to let go of older relationships that are no longer sustainable in order to create space, time and available attention for new ones.

> ## TIPS
>
> - If you had a very good relationship and lots of common ground, don't despair if you suddenly find yourself thinking about your future from the outer cold zone. A close friend of mine remarked that she found it difficult, almost impossible, to think of how she could love her partner again. A week later, they had both found their way back into shared territory and the feelings returned. Love doesn't go away so quickly. For good reasons, love is deeply etched. The same is true of deep friendships.
> - Whilst you may be familiar with a large number of people, it is foolish to assume you have lots of friends. Remember that we can only maintain a limited number of true, deep friendships.

Uses

Negotiation, conflict management and in thinking through friendships, alliances, acquaintances and any important relationship at home or work. Avoiding complacency. Keeping real friendships alive by remembering obligations to others include more than 'transactions'.

Further Reading

See Shakespeare's plays. See Chaucer's *Canterbury Tales*.

For further material on conflict and negotiation, and additional practitioner guidelines, visit **http://www.spreid.com/book**

Winning Philosophies

Module 22

Self-awareness

This is an immensely important skill. Self-awareness opens the door to higher levels of performance. If this door remains closed, then you seriously limit what you are capable of. Self-awareness magnifies the impact of any of the tips, tools and techniques you may decide to use.

Without doubt, in order to upgrade and advance your thinking and generate higher levels of performance in your life, you need to be truly self-aware. This skill, balanced with sufficient confidence, is THE gateway to higher performance. Without self-awareness, all the other skills become mere tricks.

What We See

If you are self-aware, taking full control and responsibility for your own thoughts, choices and actions becomes easier. Let's use an analogy as a creative thinking tool to illustrate my point. Consider control of a car. As a car driver you need to:

- Be alert, pay attention to the vehicle, know that you are actually in your car and not on a boat, truck or a plane.
- Be aware of where you are, the immediate conditions around you and what is coming toward you.
- Know where the car's controls are.
- Know what all of the controls actually do.
- Understand what the car is capable of in different conditions.
- Be aware of the impact of the car on other people.

Using this analogy of 'control of a car' we can infer that the same rules outlined above apply to you and the control and direction of your mind.

If you are NOT responsible for steering your own mind, then who or what will steer your journey in life? It is possible to direct your own thoughts and feelings. Once in control, you can begin to employ alternative mental models and templates that smart people use to produce better results. Self-awareness magnifies what you are capable of.

What to Do

Each of us is born with choice. Choose to switch on self-awareness. Simply pay more attention to yourself. Be aware of your body and your mind.

Pay attention to what is happening inside you, as well as around you.

Actually, the simplest way to start to develop self-awareness is to think only about how you are breathing. As you try to focus only on breathing in and out you may notice lots of thoughts and sensations clamouring to be heard and given attention. Rather than fighting them off, choose to be aware of their presence but also choose to remain centred on just appreciating each breath. If you do this for 15 minutes in the evening and 15 minutes in the morning you will, after a few short sessions, find you are becoming more relaxed and centred.

When we relax our bodies, we are more able to relax our minds and gain a better level of awareness. Mind and body are connected as one. It is foolish to think of mind and body as separate.

As you become more self-aware, it is important to view matters as they are, in a dispassionate way, rather than seeing an accumulation of challenges or 'threats'. Even if you initially do not like what you find in any given situation, you can, by being self-aware, choose your reaction and you can choose to think and act positively.

- You will need to develop a sense of patience with yourself once you become aware of the clamour for attention of your thoughts and sensations. If you can learn this, you may find patience with others too.

- As a useful side-effect of taking care to 'listen to yourself' you will increase your readiness and skill for listening to other people. Listening well is of tremendous value if you are to get what you want from life.

- Self-awareness ensures you are aware of your 'total self', meaning you are aware of your mind, your body, your thoughts and your feelings all in real time, in the moment.

- Being self-aware means you are much more conscious of your thoughts, your choices, your interactions and the consequences of your actions.

- Self-observation in real time provides lots of healthy feedback and a solid basis for continuous self-development.

- Gaining self-awareness is a step toward gaining control of yourself and some, if not all, of your situation.

Why This Is Important

Self-awareness gives us better opportunities to learn and develop.

TIPS

- Be self-aware as often as you can.
- Without self-awareness, we may stumble blindly or be led by others who may or may not have our best interests at heart.
- There is a level of personal awareness that is appropriate to our situation.
- Part of the skill of gaining self-awareness is letting go of the clamour for attention of things past, of things future and of things that are distractions or illusions.

Use

In any conscious or physical process where you seek to improve.

Overuse

Self-indulgence, introspection, a lack of outward-facing action. Should be held in proportion and in balance with a reasonable amount of confidence, optimism and due concern for other lives around you.

Next Steps

Observe yourself in action. Keep doing it.

Last Words

Instead of just thinking clearly about what we want, we need to turn thoughts into action and productive behaviour. Self-awareness leads to choices. You can choose to change, if you want to. You can develop choices on how you will improve yourself, but nothing substantial will happen until you choose to act.

Further Activity and Reading

There are lots of self-help, philosophical texts available, as well as a variety of religious books on self-awareness. Look for work that will build self-confidence alongside self-awareness. Yoga, stretch and meditation classes can help. Some of the martial arts guide people in self and spatial awareness; the rituals, physical training and practice also create a sense of self-security and confidence that need not manifest in violent acts.

Module 23

A Relative Philosophy

We hold information in our minds in a relative way.

If you want to adapt or change your view of reality, consider adjusting how your mind holds and values the relationships between information. Then consider how you create relative judgements.

For example: is the person, job, lifestyle, money, sex, holiday you held to be 'great', truly great or are you holding up an illusion? Is the person, the house, the place, the experience, the client, the friendship, the marriage, the garden actually so bad or are you making unrealistic comparisons, or comparing with the wrong benchmarks.

What you are feeling relative to what you are thinking is important too. A mismatch needs close attention at a deeper level.

Sometimes we change, expecting something better, but then find that we are actually no better off. If that is the case, we were either unfortunate or we misjudged ourselves or something along the way.

Being aware of why we hold information in our minds in a particular way may tell us something about the way we form our personal judgements and values.

Adjusting your judgements and personal benchmarks by which you decide how you will 'be' requires high levels of self-awareness.

Module 24

Estimates, Prediction, Projection and Reality

We began this section of the book with a picture of a fish that I used to show how prior knowledge gets in the way sometimes. Despite this, we still need sufficient information to help us make judgements and to foresee what might happen next. For example, as adults we know that if we step in front of fast moving vehicles we will be hurt or that if we drive faster than a speed limit there will be consequences. We continue to estimate, project and predict.

The ability to estimate what might happen next is important. To some extent, the further into the future you are able to accurately predict and prepare for future events may be an indication of intelligence.

The disciplined process of logic allows us to make simple predictions based on processes we understand. When we know a little maths, we can predict that one plus one equals two. This simple level of predictive ability depends on the information we have stored. We learn cause and effect are linked. So, for example, if we take out an 'easy' credit facility or loan we ought to know we will have to pay it back, with costs later. In some cases, some people see the ease of obtaining money but then fail to connect the consequences of the need to pay the money back. The manner of their reasoning may be flawed in that they:

- are not capable of following the logic of cause and effect
- engage a mental process of denial of present reality
- fail to make a good estimate of relative worth or risks
- demonstrate a total lack of imagination about the consequences of their actions

Good mental logic requires discipline, but in order to make reasonable projections we also require at least a little imagination about value and consequences going forward in time.

'Live now and don't worry about tomorrow' can be a quick route to becoming a beggar.

A firm grip on reality is another important aspect of our ability to perform well. This is particularly important in a world where there is a high level of seductive illusion. Our grasp of reality depends upon how well we perceive the world as it exists 'here and now', as opposed to how we would like or imagine it to be. For example, the popular media bombards our minds with products we must have in order to be complete/accepted/worthwhile or happy.

Here and Now Estimates

Our grasp of reality depends on an ability to be disciplined about cause and effect and how realistic our estimates of the future are.

Possession of a realistic grasp on reality as it exists 'here and now' determines how well we perform. For example, I once saw a 40-year-old father who thought he was in control. He clearly believed he had the authority and sufficient ability to challenge an uncouth youth regarding unwanted attention toward his teenage daughter. The older man got badly thumped as a consequence of challenging the younger man. The older man had a poor estimate of himself and of what was likely to happen next. From time to time, it is wise to review how we make estimates and the assumptions we base these on.

In summary, then, increasing your ability to think and behave in a higher performance way at this level involves gaining:

- experience and information
- access to a variety of basic mental models and filters
- discipline and improved logical ability
- at least a little imagination
- at least a little ability to predict

You will have ascended to territory two if you have developed sufficient self-awareness. Your ability to build progress within the second territory will, however, depend upon additional skills.

Territory Two

Light Fog and Uncertain Ground

Break-out and Upgrade

One significant defining upgrade from Territory One to Two is the ability to let go of the idea that the world is about 'absolutes' and to see things in a relative way. Territories Two, Three and Four have one characteristic in common. They involve progressively increasing levels of ambiguity. With increasing ambiguity comes decreasing certainty. What differentiates Territory One from Territory Two ability is the extent to which a person can:

- **tolerate uncertainty**
- retain a degree of **self-confidence** whilst having
  - moderate **self-awareness**
  - awareness of imposed and imagined **boundaries**
  - a wider range of **models** and intellectual tools AND
  - the ability to **synthesise** original ideas to almost complete pragmatic solutions

In order to cope you will need a variety of skills. We will cover each of these upgrades in turn.

Once you are reasonably competent with the skills in the previous section and have *also* acquired some sense of self-awareness you are probably already beginning to operate within Territory Two.

Your ability to get the best out of your thought process depends on what you perceive. A major upgrade in the way you think involves the extent to which you are aware of what you think you perceive as reality in terms of where you place or perceive 'boundaries'. Some of these boundaries you impose on yourself, whilst others are created or influenced by external factors. These boundaries link to your sense of confidence as well as your orientation toward certainty and ambiguity.

The certainty funnel shown in 'Useful Models and Tools' will help you 'see' where you are in terms of your orientation and your journey. The journey will take a lot longer than it takes to read this book. Not everyone wishes to or is capable of travelling through Territories Three and Four because of the increasingly high levels of uncertainty involved. From here on up any upgrade to the way you think and behave involves more feeling and higher personal awareness. **But** the journey toward higher levels of personal performance stops right here and all the tips and tools in the book are devalued to mere 'tricks' if you are not yet self-aware.

Upgrade Your Models and Tools

Module 25

A Sense of Certainty

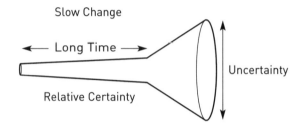

Possession of a sense of certainty really matters. If you feel secure you can think clearly. If you are uncertain, then doubts may drain your energy unless you have either an effective coping mechanism in place or a higher level of tolerance for uncertainty.

In order to perform effectively at higher levels you may need to increase your comfort level regarding increased uncertainty and ambiguity.

We can crudely plot tolerance for certainty within a range of boundaries using the illustration above.

Different people have different levels of tolerance for certainty. For example, some people need a strict routine to live by, where most things and people in their lives follow a clearly defined schedule. In contrast, other people prefer more liberty in what they do and take a looser approach to how they form their thoughts.

What We See

This model uses the inside of a funnel shape to illustrate differing levels of certainty. On the left there is only a small amount of variation and on the right there is a lot. At any given point, people with different tolerance levels will experience 'certainty' in different ways.

We can use this particular shape in several ways:

- as a static model to describe how people see their boundaries at a fixed point in time
- to describe the passage of time and how uncertainty levels can change in different ways over time
- to describe the different directions people travel in

Interestingly, we can interpret two different perceptions by assuming reality is read from left to right – or – is read from right to left. For example, many of us believe we live in the logical, relatively predictable world on the left. In this case, time passes from the relatively certain present on the left-hand side of the funnel toward an unknown future on the right open neck of the funnel. A smaller number of people, however, view reality from the right to the left. They see chaos all around them and seek to drive sense out of nonsense and ultimately rigorous, well-bounded rules and procedures – or reality, as the rest of us would see it. In effect, this latter group of people are those who would like to, or who actually do, shape our world.

For those of us who see the world working from left to right, our near future, as far as we choose to see, looks quite predictable, known and reasonably certain. On the left the degree of likely variation is relatively low and the outer boundaries are quite close together. As we move toward our future on the right-hand side of this model the boundaries widen and the level of actual uncertainty increases.

This basic left to right funnel model was originally devised by planners working with insurance companies to determine their mathematical probability calculations for assessing different sorts of risks, such as heart attacks, car accidents involving 18-year-olds, floods, or any other calamity they might insure against. If the actuaries who used this approach were correct in their estimates, then their companies placed their bets in a relatively safe way and stayed in business.

For those of us working left to right in our work or personal lives, the long term might be regarded as quite stable, with very low likelihood of change any time soon. Our view of the world would be self-assured. Our mental model would be reflected in the long perception funnel shape shown above. However, not everyone's future is so predictable and steady. Some people experience or seek out, environments in which change is much more likely in the short term, as illustrated by the much shorter funnel shown below. The journey from left to right is still the same, but the transition speed is much faster.

What Is Long-term?

We see different shaped perception funnels operating in different organisations too. For example, people working within a water utility or construction company might be generally disposed to take a very long view as to the rate of change in their environment represented by the illustration above. By contrast, a high-technology manufacturer may regard 'long-term' as months and a city trader operating on the money market may regard long-term in minutes. This shorter view of 'reality' may be more accurately described by the illustration below.

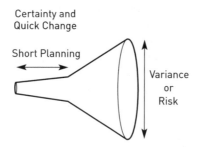

Each organisation operates within a different 'climate' as indicated by the different shaped funnels.

Certainty and Systems Evolution

The prevailing rate of change will create a pattern of decisions and behaviours AND an equivalent pattern of people and systems will evolve into roles and behaviours that fit this need. Individuals, systems and organisations evolve gradually and align according to their particular experience of risk and rates of change. In other words, your individual perceptions and those of your immediate group or organisation will tend to co-evolve.

Along the way, you shape the environment you choose to be within and the environment, in turn, shapes you.

What you think you 'see' may of course be either right or wrong from someone else's perspective. In essence, that is a central problem with perception. What I 'see' is not always what you 'see'.

What to Do

- Try to get to know the shape of the reality funnel you're in.
- Is the particular risk profile of your funnel stable?
- What would change the shape of the funnel?
- Are you expecting the whole shape of the funnel to be changed in some way?
- Have you ever tried, tolerated or learned from the opposite 'funnel journey' to the one you most often use?

TIP

- Remember the shapes of the funnels are likely to evolve and change over time. Slow-change funnels may evolve to become fast-change funnels, whilst fast ones could evolve into long steady patterns. They can also begin anew and, of course, simply fall apart.

Uses

Dealing with change. Strategic planning.

Additional practitioner guidelines are available at **http://www.spreid.com/book**

Further Reading

See later section combining frames of reference and the funnel. This second combined model creates a powerful insight into decision-making, different ways of
having fun, and problems with leadership, change and innovation. See also Sandy
Dunlop's book, *Business Heroes*, Capstone, 1997, for helpful insights based on
heroic legends.

Module 26

Dreamer/Critic/Realist

Walt Disney is said to have intuitively used a dynamic pattern of thinking to drive the success of his ideas. What the model above shows us is that in order to rise up the thinking/doing performance scale, we need to have at our disposal the flexibility and ability to employ different ways of thinking to get results.

This thinking pattern can produce results from an individual, a family and a team. When one individual is able to integrate all three of these skills at speed we see a higher order of thinking – **original synthesis** (see next module). Teams can achieve this higher level of performance, albeit at a slower speed, by acquiring the individual skills and adopting this pattern of thinking.

What We See

American authors Dilts, Epstein and Dilts, in their book, *Tools for Dreamers*, describe Walt Disney's thinking style. According to these authors, he successfully used three thought styles, described as dreamer, realist and critic. This pattern coincides with two of the fundamental thinking pathways in the following way:

1 Critic = Focused, Converging Thinking
2 Dreamer = Uninhibited Creative, Wide Divergent Thinking
+ a third practical level, called 'Realist' = how can this be made to work

Integrating these three patterns in your mind can lead to **original synthesis** – novel, original ideas and processes that work in practice.

According to the authors, Disney managed to throw himself passionately into one of these roles for the duration of a working meeting and then leave. Importantly, before major projects were undertaken, Walt would ensure that the three styles, dreamer/critic/realist, had each been fully engaged, often **more than once**, until the basic elements of a new idea sat comfortably in all three realms. In other words, the persistent challenge was to find a great idea that retained high levels of novelty AND would stand up to critical analysis AND remained realistic.

My experience of leading several thousand people through creative thinking skills workshops is that most people expect quick easy answers and will often give up too soon.

This simple model demonstrates that it is rare to get a fully functional working idea in one simple flash of inspiration.

Also, I have noticed that there are plenty of people capable of generating ideas but there seem to be fewer people who can turn ideas into reality. There are a few 'dreamers who do' and 'lots of dreamers who don't'.

The Walt Disney model is my favourite because it sums up what is needed to bring new ideas into reality.

What to Do

- Be clear about what you believe you need.
- Does this subject require more critical or more realistic thinking or is the 'dream' or imagination element lacking? Make sure that the thinking is given a clear and detailed direction.
- Make sure you are aware of how different people prefer to think in the group dealing with the subject in hand.
- Are your colleagues predominantly critics, dreamers or realists? If there are any ability gaps, fill them.
- Get training for the whole group in all three disciplines.
- Arrange your time and meetings to ensure that when dealing with the birth of a new idea all three realms are each visited several times.

Why This Is Important

This pattern is simple and embraces the major domains that need to be covered to develop anything that needs to be seen as well-rounded. 'Dreamer/critic/realist' is a much warmer description of the divergent and convergent modes of thinking and is much more likely to be remembered.

> Smart people find a thinking template first and then process their thoughts through it.

TIP

- For some people, flipping between different thinking paths can be confusing, so call a break in meetings where a change of thinking style and direction is required. Then set the scene so people can orientate and engage with the direction you set.

Use

This is an all-round reality check that can be applied literally to anything you do in all walks of life. It asks three simple questions of you.

1 Am I/are we being creative enough?
2 What must I/we do to make this really work in the real world?
3 What could go wrong; what would critics say?

Use the model in relationships at any level, look at work at any stage, and consider your purchases and life decisions. This model applies across a wide spectrum of possibilities, because it represents a fundamental cornerstone of human thought.

Additional exercises and practitioner guidelines are available at **http://www.spreid. com/book**

References to the man Walt Disney are based upon comments in an NLP practitioners' book, *Tools for Dreamers*, by Dilts, Epstein and Dilts, Meta Publications, California 95014, 1991; pages 6–7. ISBN 0916990 26 5

Module 27

Original Synthesis

The ability to synthesise original thoughts is a key step up the intellectual ladder.

When working at Territory One ability, we saw that there were two major directions that our thinking may follow. Combining a moderate amount of focus with just a small amount of creative thinking creates a Territory One 'realist'. A higher level of performance comes from someone who has successfully integrated the two major thinking pathways. They can very quickly perform a full divergent spread of thinking and then, in fractions of a second, integrate multiple possibilities, reducing and improving them to a few novel, yet pragmatic solutions.

> **Original synthesis** is clearly a higher order of mental processing than that possessed by a 'realist'.

What We See

In between the two major thinking patterns of narrow focus and wide divergent thinking is a place in the mind where some constraints exist. Here we find creative ideas being turned into something practical, but the process involves a considerable sense of tension generated between the demands to intellectually 'play' and 'focus' at the same time, thereby pulling in opposite directions. Tolerance of this disruptive energy helps produce novel ideas. Increasing your tolerance also helps to create a space in the mind for another skill used in Territory Three, involving keeping two contradictory ideas alive.

What to Do

Practice using both creative and focused thinking techniques. The more practice you have, the more likely it is that you will be able to integrate the two. The key upgrade step is the integration. The aim in the synthesis phase of thinking is to stay open enough to allow in moderate amounts of new thinking AND at the same time to hunt for new pragmatic solutions. This requires a suspension of judgement as well as sensitivity to boundaries and constraints. In summary, consolidation, improvement and review without decision happen within the 'synthesis' pattern.

Uses

Innovation and entrepreneurial development of ideas. Advanced problem-solving.

Modules 28 to 31 Using Curves and Waves: The Truth

Albert Einstein is said to have imagined what it would be like to travel sitting on the tip of a beam of light. Clearly he was NOT just relying on everyday linear logic. He used this idea and other thought experiments to help his mind develop ground-breaking advances in physics.

The following modules each contain lessons in their own right but, more importantly, I want to convey the idea that you might 'shape what is happening' to create your own models and impressions in your mind by using, in this case, a variety of wave-like pictures. My intention is to convey the relative nature of things and that absolute positions are not so common.

Module 28

Curved Truths

Uncovering Patterns Within Our Own Big Pictures

How it is

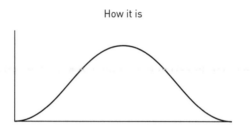

In reality things, issues, people, processes, etc., tend to follow patterns and trends. At a higher level of awareness, in viewing 'reality' from a suitable distance, you may notice that not everything falls neatly into 'absolutes'. You may then notice that quite a few subjects demonstrate a distribution of some sort. An even distribution might be represented by a 'bell curve' shape, such as the one above. Such a curve can help you think about a 'distribution of sense'.

There is often a gradient, a curve or a wave to life that can be mapped and tapped. If you can see this as part of a bigger picture, you may gain an insight or an advantage.

What We See

As individual fashions, ambitions, products, companies and even nation states rise and fall over time, this shape also helps remind us of the position of events along a 'life cycle' that follows some sort of shape. All things live and die, eventually. The irony is that in our early careers and relationships we never think of ourselves as riding a bell curve. Perhaps we only choose to see the 'up' gradient. By being too close to our challenges, we might not see the whole curve and instead see only part of the gradient. Mentally standing back helps us gain a better perspective. From a distance, we can determine the shape of the whole situation and see where best to place our efforts and what sort of results we might expect along the curve. For example, are you managing a situation that is going up or going down? Most managers aspire to 'growth' situations; however, quite different skills and expectations are required when managing a protracted decline. How will you and others be motivated during a prolonged decline?

How Scientists Use a Bell Curve

A 'bell curve' is used by all sorts of scientists to see if an event is a chance occurrence or something genuinely different. If the incidence of things is evenly distributed, the shape of the graph reflects this and is described as a 'normal distribution curve'. For example, population height on the horizontal axis versus the incidence on the vertical axis would tell us something about population height. Very few people are really small (left-hand 'tail' of the graph) and very few people are very tall (right-hand tail of the graph); most people fall in the middle zone. What this shape of graph tells the scientists is that interesting things happen at the edges, or at the extremes. We'd expect to find, in this example, as many giants as we find dwarves.

However, as a thinking tool, I am not so much interested in numbers, but more in the underlying principles. Curves like these tell us that once we know the general shape of things, it is only the edges that hold the interesting exceptions. What occurs in the middle is usual, there is lots of it and it is much more predictable. Remember, in evolutionary terms, new species emerge from the edges, the most demanding margins.

If you are trying to shape an argument or to innovate, look to the 'truths' at the edges.

What to Do

Think about and roughly plot your personal positions in life, in relationships, in jobs. Plot your product, your work relationships and your industry on the bell curve. Then plot the position of your economy, then the macro economy. Where are these bits of information all pointing? How fresh or tired are your relationships and networks? Are you/your industry/the wider context on the way up or the way down? Management of a falling, descending set of circumstances is quite different from an ascent.

At work, if the longer view is looking tough, sometimes it is important to get out before there is a rush for the door. Plan your exit strategy. Alternatively, secure a guaranteed golden exit package early on. If you've spotted a marvellous growth opportunity, get in as early as possible and ride it on up.

Why This Is Important

The graph reminds us 'what goes up, comes down'. If you are in the wrong place at the wrong time at the wrong age, if you experience the sudden demise of an industry or the loss of a key relationship (for example, a mentor or sponsor), these misfortunes (or poorly adopted positions) can set you back substantially in your sense of security, your career and your relationships.

Use

To produce alert career, product, life and strategic planning.

Overuse

Sometimes it is more enlightening to go with the flow. You cannot plan everything. Trying to see too far ahead, you might actually miss the show.

Module 29

Clarity and Truth

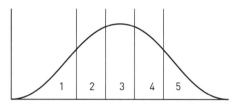

What is true? When our world turns 'foggy', what constitutes 'truth' may be dependent on context and interpretation. Many of us have an incomplete appreciation of the difference between absolute truth and relative truth. A partitioned bell curve can be used to improve our understanding of the foggy world of relative truths.

For example, what would you consider excessive entertaining? Where is the deciding line between what is expected and using entertainment as a bribe?

A bell curve model divided out as above can help us visualise different interpretations of 'the truth' across a range of possibilities. This model represents a continuous series of individual situations, in which the truth can be viewed relatively, according to context.

What We See

Our business and personal lives are full of blurred, grey areas. In a complex, fast-moving world, the truth can be difficult to think about and locate. In spite of this, we are frequently expected to produce reasonable decisions and develop a plan of action despite incomplete information or with erroneous interpretations as to what is 'true'. It can be problematic making decisions, setting targets and managing expectations when important information seems to be ambiguous. This partitioned bell curve can help us see how the truth maps out in the face of ambiguous information.

When someone tells us the answer to a question is, 'It depends,' then we would want to know, 'On what?' If the truth followed some sort of pattern we would want to understand how the pattern worked. So the next few curvy examples are intended to help you determine what might be true or reasonable.

> *History should be read with care.*
> *The victor writes and controls the stories.*

What to Do

Consider what the scales are, then divide a bell curve and slot perceptions of truth into compartments over a range of possibilities. We can then look at truth in a relative way. Here I have divided the curve in the illustration above into five zones.

Let us say that 'cheap' is represented by Zone 1 and that the scale progresses up to 'expensive' as represented by Zone 5. The vertical scale is simply the number of people undertaking the sort of activity we are mapping. So our chart shows most people operating in Zones 2, 3 and 4.

By contrasting the extremes of Zone 5 with those of Zone 1 we can demonstrate the clash between **simple logic**, where we expect consistency and uniformity, and **relative reasoning**, where a degree of elasticity is expected.

EXAMPLE

Let us consider the question of business entertaining. At what point does entertaining a business guest become a crude bribe?

A wealthy person takes an employee of another organisation to lunch. Both are very busy and both see working over lunch as an efficient use of time. So far, so good.

However, a meal in a restaurant of a capital city can cost $20, $50, $80, $120, $250, $500, or well over $5,000. The meeting is to discuss business and we should be aware that the employee is able to trade with the host.

What level of entertaining is inappropriate, especially if there is a lot at stake? The answer is, 'It depends'. For instance, if the client being entertained is the governor of the World Bank and the host the Sultan of Brunei, either might be offended if lunch is a street vendor's hamburger and a tin of fizzy lemonade; whereas a buyer from a small company might consider an entertainment value of $500 over-indulgent and excessive.

Where we call the limit on 'reasonable entertainment expenses' is a matter of context. What is right and appropriate in one domain may be totally wrong in another. The limits, the truths are relative.

EXAMPLE

To illustrate the point further, in a court case at the close of the twentieth century, a British judge in a UK court ruled that a claim for £50,000 was excessive for the redecoration of the walls of five rooms in a London apartment that had been allegedly spoiled by a tenant. The judge cut the award for Lady X to 'only' £30,000! Clearly we are in Zone 5 here!

The 'truth of the matter' often is relative. Truth depends upon context and judgement. The answer to, 'What is the truth here?' often is, 'It depends.'

Statisticians find unusual events not in the main body but at the edges of current reality. This is as true in evolutionary terms as it is with innovation, and to some extent the search for novelty in our personal lives. Look to the fringe of life, but take care not to tip over the edge. Often relationships can be improved by looking at the minor details at the edges. Little things can take upon themselves disproportionate importance: e.g., who squeezes the toothpaste 'the wrong way' or who buys who flowers and why.

TIPS

- Try to get the bigger picture before you come to conclusions, and certainly before you act. Step back and view the range of issues of a similar type across a spectrum of possibilities. Consider as many questions as you can in order to create a framework for how things may turn out. For example:

- Who has prior, recent, involved experience in this area? What was the outcome? What does he advise?

- Can you identify what factors change the nature of a judgement as circumstances change?

- Consider who is making the judgements and what influences his way of thinking.

- Given that this is an ambiguous environment, what alternatives are your adversaries prepared to base their decisions on?

- What would make people making the judgement change their minds?

- In particular, how are exceptional circumstances described?

- What is truly volatile in your case and how much influence does this volatility have on any decision?

- Who or what would change who the decision-makers are?

- Would the new decision-makers follow old or new rules and how would these potential changes affect you?

- When in a conflict or a negotiation, consider which zone a person is operating from. Look at the assets they may gamble to create a truth that others will accept. Is it cheaper to walk away?

Expectations of Fairness and the Truth in Conflict

So few things in life are absolute. 'The truth' is very much a matter of interpretation and may depend upon who is imparting the story of events. What you think and believe to be 'the truth' can ultimately become a question of who has the most money to spend. The most money often buys the most capable mind of a person who can shape information to their version of reality and who can go on to convince a judge or jury that their view is the truth. Anyone going to prove a point in a court of law should abandon all rational hope at the door for this reason.

Uses

Coming to terms with vague truths. Locating interesting precedents, exceptions or new evolutionary species and ideas. In innovation, understanding conflict and negotiation. Looking at the two fringe extremes to describe the exceptions from the norm. Creating novelties.

Further Reading

Some of us may be led to believe that justice is logical and impartial, as it should be. However, if we live in a society in which the most money buys the best minds, it might be argued that nothing much has changed since the traditions of ancient Greek sophists that Socrates would have known and suffered.

See Bertrand Russell's, *A History of Western Philosophy*, and in particular his notes on Epicurus, Plato, Aristotle and Socrates. The importance of Socrates' way of thinking to Western civilisation, and his demise, make for a good case study on the birth of reasoning, social skills and the consequences of 'success'. See also Aristotle's *Ethics*. (Several translations are available.)

Module 30

Alternative Truths

Absolute Truth, Relative Truth and Bias

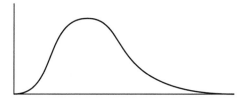

There are absolute truths, relative truths and partial truths. We should be able to distinguish which sort of 'truth' we are dealing with or seeking to create.

For example, my height is 1 m 85 cm. That is absolutely true – today. But then someone says, 'You are tall.' Is that true? The answer is, 'It depends compared to whom or what.' Relative to Scandinavian youths, I'm probably less than average. In the tall argument, there is some truth, but it is not so absolute. Relative truths are context-dependent and open to some interpretation and bias.

What We See

Real life is rarely static, absolute, or pure. Nature seems to like it that way. If perceived reality is constantly being adjusted, why should we expect our sense of what is the truth be any different? It would be wise, then, to test our 'truths' on a regular basis.

> *An absolute truth cannot be denied but a relative truth is only true in particular situations.*

Bias and the Truth

A woman who possesses $60,000 may be considered rich in a very poor country, but unexceptional if she lives in North America. In one country, she is at one end of the scale, yet she is at the opposite end of the wealth distribution curve of another, richer country. Mathematicians use these curves to tell them to pay attention to something when it does not fit the usual pattern. Cold facts, such as possessing $60,000, or being a certain height mean nothing until they are put into the right kind of context.

A normal distribution curve or bell curve is evenly balanced. Not all situations are quite so evenly spread. Sometimes the bell curve may be pushed to the left or to the right of centre by some kind of bias. Distribution of the 'facts' or 'the truth' is then 'skewed' one way or the other. What is now considered 'normal' within the sample is skewed away from what might have been expected within an even distribution.

Take wealth distribution as an example. The curve for wealth distribution could be evenly spread in some countries under a normal distribution curve, whilst in others the shape of curve may be heavily skewed toward poverty. In a few rare cases the bias is toward people being mostly wealthy, relative to other countries.

> *In thinking skills terms, when looking for a 'truth' you may choose to be aware of the presence of bias, with or without judgement.*

Being **either** 'right' **or** 'wrong' may depend upon a particular context or an interpretation at a given time. At one time in history, an English monarch had to abdicate to marry a divorcee. Some years later, society seems more relaxed about such matters, and the same ancient texts are interpreted in a very different way, allowing a prince to remain within the monarchy and marry a divorcee.

Truth and Scale

A man murders another man. Clearly it is true that he is guilty of the crime of murder in that country or place. Any accomplice who facilitates entry to the premises where the killing took place is guilty too. But if a tribal raiding party is involved and they gain facilitated entry to a palace and slaughter the present ruling family to take over a whole country – is that right or wrong in that country? What is 'true' is dependent on who is holding the rulebook, and on scale. If a wider power fails to intervene, then several murders are classed differently. Instead of being tried and jailed, the new tribe have wealth and control. Here we see a distinction between knowledge of a truth and the exercise of judgement concerning right and wrong.

What to Do

Look for the bigger picture. If the truth is open to interpretation, get as many interpretations as you can. Anything that is open to interpretation remains open to rebuttal. Look especially at the margins and for bias. The passage of time and the formation of 'unprecedented' new contexts can arise, be invented or created; given the right conditions, as we saw in the example of the raiding party, you may be able to rewrite the rulebook.

Why This Is Important

We make 'sense' in a relative way. The truth is often relative to context and to what is considered 'normal'. 'Normal' sits in the body of a map of the distribution of things. Different graph shapes can provide alternative ways of reasoning within ambiguous environments. Once we understand where we are within the whole map we can see where information 'sits' relative to other similar information. Consequently, this can help our interpretation of a good answer relative to a bad one, within some sort of context.

When it comes to a conflict or a legal contest *many people will invest high levels of emotion and cash in a particular truth, without first understanding whether or not their truth is absolute or only partially so.* In considering the relative position of truth, we can also put our expectations into an appropriate context.

Also, if we understand the overview of the total cluster of information, we are in a better position to think about unusual situations within the cluster. We can then do what our minds are best arranged for: we can manage by exception.

Uses

Reviewing reality. Decision-making. Debate and reasoning. Changing the game and creating new rules. Placing bets.

Last Words

When trying to deal with the truth of an issue and stepping back to get a better view, will you judge:

- the issue
- the context
- the times
- the scale
- the prevailing bias
- or any combination of these?

Module 31

Riding the Sine Waves

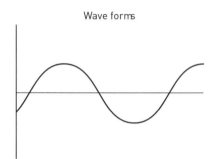

Wave forms

Events often demonstrate an ebb and flow. We should look for two things: the internal rhythms and the external cycles. We can easily see the more obvious cyclical rises and falls, but we may miss the slower cycles. Beware slow change; insipid, deadly trends creep up and get you when you are unaware! Then it is too late to act. For example, a 30-year price-plus-quality program can build into something formidable with quite modest annual targets. Internally, we can work without respite, gradually draining our physical and psychological batteries so that after 10 or 15 years we end up trying, but are unable to perform at peak performance levels. It is dangerous to be blind to the patterns that hold sway over our lives. Mapping how things rise and fall over time can be very helpful.

> For example, in the 1970's in England, students received government grants to attend university. Thirty years later a socialist government has gradually introduced and implemented a system under which students now pay their own grants AND their tuition fees. Most now leave university in debt. Whilst the policy switch was not unnoticed, it was long and slow and was eventually exhausted in the media. Because the change was gradual people accepted it.
>
> Also, in my youth, most dental treatment for the whole population was free via our health system. As a result of a government squeeze on funding for dentists, the majority of English public sector dentists have, over the last ten years, gone into private practice. In England, I now have to pay for what was once 'free'. The original policy of free health care, like higher education, is being slowly nudged back.

What We See: Insipid Change

This model differs from a static graph, which describes either a distribution of something or one turn of a particular single cycle. A regular sine wave describes the recurring, cyclical nature of something. A sine wave is curvy and continuous. It is also an engineer's way of representing a circle in a linear way. A sine wave describes a situation of 'what goes around comes around'. I like to think of sine wave images as being much more like snakes; some are fast and some are slow. The fast-moving trends you can usually see or hear; they frighten you and you react! But the slow ones can be quiet and deadly. The key learning point is that the rhythm of these snake-like waves may be so long and slow that we miss them unless we look closely.

Internal Rhythmic Waves

Rhythmic waves apply to life. We all have rhythms. We sleep, eat and drink in a particular way. Our personal energy follows a rhythm too: our bodies have a rhythm, and the way our minds work and then rest has a rhythm as well. Life has a beat, a rhythm. There are events and forces at work around us that we may see, take for granted or miss altogether. Be aware of the rhythms within yourself and the context.

The Rhythm of Love

In our most personal relationships, being in love does not always mean being in harmony. Being out of step with the rhythms of one's partner may not necessarily mean being out of love with one another either. So don't rush off and see a lawyer at the first downturn. Things tend to follow the wave – up, then down, then back up again. Divorce, or for that matter 'cheating', can be a path down, further down still and then seriously out of the game.

It is possible that 'love' exists in waves and is more available or less available to our partners depending on how much energy or compassion we are able to offer at any particular time. 'Lucky in love' might mean having two people's waves or rhythms moving more of the time in harmony.

Shakespeare waxed eloquent on how the course of true love never runs straight. In real life, we need to accept that there will be low points that need to be worked on, where we can resolve differences, forgive mistakes, grow and move on up again. The nature of love itself may change too.

When we are well, we tend not to pay attention to these 'rhythmic events and forces'. They may seem unimportant or are taken for granted, but when we are ill or our company is sick, or when we need to push for higher performance, these rhythms take on a higher significance.

If you behave according to a particular pattern that has a rhythm to it then there will be motivation or driving forces in operation. It would be wise for us to understand what these forces are and how they effect us. The shape and form of sine waves or long waves can help us think about the behaviour of events over the longer term, revealing both problems and opportunities at work and in our personal lives.

What to Do

The trick with sine waves is to recognise the frequency at which things come around again. We each have a biological cycle and our moods and abilities fluctuate. We can spot short dramatic cycles, but are not so sharp with longer rhythms. The trouble with long waves is we forget earlier pattern events. Watch out especially for slow, small, incremental changes. Each step may seem trivial and not so important; however, incremental change is additive and works in a compounding way. Over the long run, the changes add up to something substantial. A few extra biscuits a day may lead to obesity. A 2% cut in costs every year will drive down your prices substantially in the long run.

Read a variety of histories. Look for patterns as opposed to the heroes and victors. Try to uncover what always seemed to happen and the general pattern that events seemed to follow. How were conditions developed so that the general context was ripe for this particular pattern to re-emerge later? Are your present successes sowing the seeds of a bigger disaster down the line? A phoenix rises from its own ashes.

TIPS

- Adopt a long-term view of your whole self and your context and the whole of 'work'.
- Learn to step back and view the whole picture.
- Know where in the picture you are now and where you are heading.
- Watch out for long-term small, slow changes.
- Adapt to or accommodate the rhythms you want and resist the ones you do not want.
- Examples to consider: the long-term trends to get rid of pensions and reduce costs, global climate change, globalisation of labour, and how often you may have to remarry and or re-skill.
- Consider your lifetime 'personal energy reserves' – how will these pan out over time?

Why This Is Important

You are either in control or you are not. Take your chances as they come or spot the major trends and get ready to surf or avoid the next wave.

Tidal Waves

There are some waves that seem to be so big we don't see them. One lesson we seemingly fail to learn is that economic recession always, always follows a boom. The Japanese stock market index defied gravity and sailed from a highly unrealistic valuation of 30,210 in December 1988 to a surreal 38,910 in December 1989. Journalists then talked of 'special circumstances' that applied to Japanese share prices. Trillions of dollars of 'value' evaporated and 15 years later, the index was still less than half the 'value' witnessed in 1989. Sadly, millions of people were seriously hurt by hyper-greed. They missed the lesson of history about change and in particular the simple equation of what goes around comes around once sufficient numbers have forgotten an old lesson. History shows us this lesson will visit us again.

Further Reading

Professor Peter F. Drucker, in *Innovation and Entrepreneurship*, gives historical examples in which mass greed (hyper-greed in my terms) created stock market booms and crashes, each with terrible consequences. Drucker also describes the speed at which emerging trends can profoundly change society. It only took Europe and America 30 years from 1830 to 1860 to make the shift from rural to city-state industrialisation. At the time of writing we are now in the middle of at least one major transformational trend. Have you spotted it?

Research Kondratiev cycles or waves (occasionally referred to as K-waves) if you are interested in long-term strategy and macro-economics. Look at long-range population demographic trends globally, alongside wealth, food and water and resource distribution. For a higher level of appreciation of complex systems that behave within repeating patterns, look at books on 'Systems Thinking'.

Module 32

Critical Life Forces Map

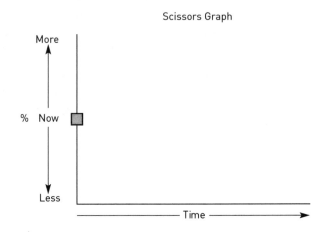

Scissors Graph

You cannot be a high-performance individual or team if you are, individually or collectively, physically or mentally ill. Demanding environments can suck energy, time, joy and life from you. Failure to routinely step back and reconsider the where, when, why, how and what of what you are doing will significantly reduce your performance because of this draining process.

You will, like everyone else, have upper tolerance limits. If you fail to acknowledge them, you may put your life at risk. People really do suffer heart attacks, mental burn-out and nervous breakdowns through overwork. This exercise shows how it can happen and makes the case that you should get smart about how you think and smart about what you will – and just as important – what you will **not do** in future.

What We See

We have two boundaries to consider here: an outer boundary regarding our perception and an inner capability boundary. If there is a problem, we need to pay attention to both. As with the health warnings on drugs, alcohol and tobacco, many people trigger a convenient denial mechanism of, 'It won't happen to me.' Overwork is not talked about enough. Any physical and mental burn-out issues are generally taboo subjects. People shy away, not knowing what to say when the person who burned out looks OK on the outside but her mind cannot summon up enough energy to make even simple decisions. Like a broken leg, a broken mind can heal, but as with a major leg fracture a mind also requires time and quite a few supports and crutches to heal and recover.

We often fail to see the bigger picture and instead look at things happening in isolation. A scissors map appears when trends fail to flow together but instead widen apart.

You really must avoid this destructive pattern.

If we use the graphing technique and we see a series of trends that are important AND they widen and open up, beware. This is a potential killer. Where the trends widen like a pair of jaws, watch out! People lose their hair, have heart attacks and burn out trying to do what they always did, but at an increasingly demanding rate.

What to Do

Map several trends regarding your work, your home life, and the demands placed upon you – including the mental, physical, economic, time and other resources you personally possess to meet these pressures.

Draw a graph on plain paper as above. The trends you draw should be over an agreed period of time. The lines you draw will be a rough approximation. Colour coding might help. Draw several lines representing several different forces on the same chart so that they overlay each other. Map several trends that are personal to you on the same chart so that you can see where and approximately when these coincide to reinforce what is happening in a positive or a negative way.

Look for situations where the trends are diverging.

The example below shows someone who is contracted to work 40 hours but 'gives' 60 hours. (As an aside, that is 50% for free, or to put it another way, nearly a 1,000 hours a year of your leisure time gifted for – what precisely?) In this example, the starting point is at 150%.

The scissors graph suggests that to maintain performance at today's levels, the work rate will have to increase. Since the lines open up without respite, more and more effort will be demanded by the system in which this person exists and works. Unless you can redirect the forces depicted by these lines, you will eventually suffer.

The only way to undo this deadly trend is to fundamentally change the way you do things AND to fundamentally change the expectations and demands of others.

TIP

- Some environments are manic and driven. Rather than fight a whole system, it is sometimes smarter to conserve your personal energy and leave to begin anew in a better place staffed by well people who operate in a good frame of mind. One step sideways, three steps forward.

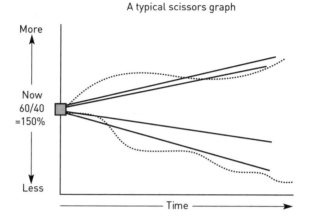

A typical scissors graph

Scissors Graph — Why This Is Important

A scissors graph will suggest that at some point a personal tolerance threshold may be breached by a series of diverging, relentless forces. You will either suffer the consequences or be driven to change in a fundamental way.

For further practical details on the model and for additional developer or trainer material, please visit **http://www.spreid.com/book**

Tuning the Controls

Module 33

Finding Outer Edges

Reality is defined by edges and boundaries. When you are looking at a thing or an issue, what is it that you believe you 'see'? And how does what you believe you are looking at influence your decisions and behaviour? If what you think you are looking at is in fact an illusion or just plain wrong, then any decisions related to what you thought you saw are likely to be wrong too. Is what you are looking at really just a problem or is it also an opportunity?

For example, some people see realistic opportunities where others only see insurmountable problems.

Your **perception** of boundaries can strongly influence your decision-making and behaviour.

Challenging what we think we see is one of several big obstacles faced by anyone dealing with complicated 'stuff'. Artists, management consultants, managers, project heads and leaders who want to think clearly need to challenge and re-check their perceptions. If they do not, their performance may be based on a wrong interpretation of reality.

What We See

As an artist and a thinker, I'm quite keen on what people call boundaries. When we take a close look at real life, there are few 'drawn edges', particularly when it comes to people, their activities and their issues. The 'edge' or the boundary is often an illusion.

There are at least two ways to define a boundary or an edge when painting. One is to take a line and paint in where you believe there is a real edge. The second way is to lay down blocks of colour or shade that describe where the light is or is not. As if by magic, what people perceive as 'edges' emerge. Many of us look at things and believe that the boundaries, the 'edges' we see are real and contain what we are looking at.

Our minds as much as our eyes shape what we see.

When I'm painting or considering something important, I find it necessary to re-define and question what I believe I see. Sometimes tight, defined focus helps, but often it's a question of widening the field of view and squinting through half-closed eyes to get the bigger 'lumps of stuff' into perspective. In other words, I reduce the detail in order to see what is there. Alternatively, sometimes things are defined by what is around them as much as their intrinsic properties. We can 'see' things in a new perspective by NOT looking directly at the subject but by looking at the surrounding issues or objects.

The exploitation of an insight for an artist or a consultant is then a matter of careful composition so that others can see what he sees.

When an artist, lover or manager tries, but fails, to challenge his own assumptions, or to 'see' where the interesting boundaries are, he ends up with something that does not have a ring of truth about it. His art, work or relationships feel incomplete or lacking vitality.

Different people draw different boundaries around what they 'see'. For example, when a group of people look at a really tall 'skyscraper' building: one simply notices a tall building; another appreciates that being so tall it must sit on some very deep, solid foundations; whilst the third, perhaps an engineer, is aware that it might have a few floors missing at the higher levels so that the wind will blow through to stop the building swaying beyond the tolerance level of its steel carcass. A fourth person might regard the building as something financial, whereas a small child might see our skyscraper as scenery for a superhero movie. Each has a partial view of the whole that in some way reflects his personal interests. Each 'edge' is seen differently.

What to Do

- Take reference points very close in and wider out than you normally would. (Use the squint trick to view only the cruder, bigger shapes.) Then have lots of practice at looking.
- View it literally upside down.
- Leave the art or the issue in a conspicuous walk-by place. An idea can catch you unawares and you may spot obvious errors when you are not looking too hard. Challenge your perceptions as to what is real now and what is likely to be real in the future.
- Check and re-check your assumptions, alignment and behaviours – what we say is not always in line with what we actually do.

Why This Is Important

It is wise to know where the edge is, lest we trip and fall over it. There are two dimensions here: an inner boundary (your personal capability limits), and a boundary of how you perceive reality – past, present and imagined in the future. (For more on personal boundaries, read the next three modules.)

Familiarity and selective perception limit our horizons. If our lenses on life are clouded, narrow or simply looking in the wrong places, we may be at risk or we miss a great opportunity. When people fail to see the bigger picture, they can make everyday tactical errors and, eventually, major strategic

---

TIPS

- Travel the boundaries as a stranger and gather knowledge and alliances. Gather resources other people can use but make sure you return home before someone else steals your throne.
- Travel anonymously, without a badge of office, when in search of new knowledge.
- See life as a small child would.

Uses

Seeing the bigger picture. Discovering useful blind spots and sensitive issues. In conflict and negotiation. As an advantage over those who cannot or fail to see boundaries.

Module 34

Detail and Blind Spots

Perception works in different ways for different people. Some people see detail, whilst many are quite literally blind to discrepancies or variations in the detail.

For example, can you see what is wrong with the image above?

A lack of attention to detail will inhibit you at some stage. Developing a coping strategy that compensates for a lack of attention to detail is vital if you want to succeed and hang on to your gains.

What We See

We possess, to differing degrees, the ability to take existing information and make predictions of what is expected. Some people use fast scanning and gather a minimum amount of detail before 'forming' a conclusion. Often they may be correct, but they can make errors, particularly when it comes to detail. For some people, when they look at something familiar they believe they see *what they expect to see*. They fail to see what is really there.

The problem for many people like me is that we believe what we are 'seeing' is true. Not everyone will have noticed the second 'in' shown in the illustration above. I belong to the group that would miss this. I'm a scanner and I don't see detail unless I really try hard to concentrate my mind. People who are very good at processing detail immediately see small errors, so they find my difficulty odd. It is dangerous to assume other people think and 'see' the way we do.

To illustrate, I once had five other senior executives sign off on an expensive print job that would be used by our sales people as competitor comparison material. All six of us missed several 25 mm text errors and the job was printed. Of course, several of our eagle-eyed sales people immediately spotted the mistakes at the launch meeting. The job had to be reprinted overnight at great expense and with great embarrassment. The shame of it all was the material was exactly what was needed but I allowed poor implementation to let me down. I'm sure that error set my career back by at least a year.

What to Do

- Get to know who are the scanners and who are the detail-spotters.
- If you are not sure if you are a 'scanner', get someone to check how long it takes you to see minor errors in detailed text.
- As a leader, make sure teams of important people are aware of who is a scanner and who spots the detail.
- Scanners may have other advantageous skills to compensate for their limitations. Capitalise on these and team them up with detail-spotters.

Why This Is Important

Groups or individuals can assume 'someone else is taking care of the detail'. That assumption is often wrong and can be both dangerous and expensive.

TIPS

- If you are a scanner, make really good friendships or alliances – contracts even – with people who clearly see detail, and make sure they check your most important work before it is released. An automated document spell-check is not at all sufficient, because one can suffer more from the incorrect placement of a word than from a spelling error.
- Detail-blindness can become a significant weakness. Blind people often have coping strategies. If you are detail-blind, make sure you know what your personal detail coping strategy is.

Uses

Quality control. High-impact projects. Anything in which many people are involved. Marketing communications. Assigning responsibility according to awareness of your own and other people's talents and limitations. Some people are great at vision, some at detail; make sure you have a mix.

Module 35

Personal Anchors

We all are 'anchored' somehow. Having some anchorage points in our lives is important. Good anchors allow us to feel secure and permit confident decision-making.

Sometimes we may feel 'hemmed in' by life and seek to break out of some sort of trap we believe we are in. If we cut our anchors, we can liberate ourselves, but we could cut too many and literally be set adrift on uncharted waters.

So, for example, if one of your big anchors is, 'My life is my job', and you are coming up to a major job change or retirement, how will you make the transition productive and enjoyable? How will you let go of old anchors and what will take their place? How will the people and issues attached to your other big anchors be affected?

If our anchors are too tight, we may sink in a storm. For example, holding on too long to a job you cannot do, or that you hate or love too much may lead to severe problems in more important aspects of your life.

Our ability to think clearly and to perform well depends on knowing what or where our personal anchors are AND having the ability to loosen, tighten, let go and replace them as needed. We may not do this often, but if we do, finding and placing new anchors should be a well-considered conscious act.

What We See

When we 'anchor' ourselves, by definition we operate within some sort of boundaries. In the absence of clear anchors and boundaries, we may feel insecure and find it difficult to think clearly and to behave in a beneficial way. Anchors provide the sense of security that is an essential foundation for human well-being and performance.

Anchors might include beliefs, values, people, loyalties, habits, objects possessions, resources, religion, philosophy, places, rituals and routines. We may stay within boundaries we create or invent. Some boundaries are true and real whilst others are imaginary, an illusion or false.

Sometimes we place the boundary anchors ourselves, close to us for comfort or seemingly far away if we desire a 'freedom' of some sort. Sometimes what we believe to be a firm boundary is nothing more than an illusion or a set of untested assumptions that can be changed.

Well-placed boundaries can facilitate day-to-day decision making. Once our anchor points are established, decisions can be made relative to these reference points.

What to Do

Anchors are many and varied. They keep you on your own idea of your personal version of the 'straight and narrow pathway between right and wrong'. Whatever your anchors are, they need to be checked out on a regular basis. Hold on to those that are good and valid, but anything that does no good should be ditched or at least reworked. Some of your deep personal anchors that include your core values are not likely to change. These are central to who you are as a person.

Get to understand what beliefs hold you in place. Write them down.

- Are the assumptions underpinning these still valid and appropriate?
- Are any of your anchors in contest with each other? What contradictions does this cause? How will you resolve, reconcile or live with these?
- What new anchors could you build to replace those that are eroding?

Why This Is Important

A sense of security is a fundamental human need. In our times of deepest need, we will turn to the people and the ideas that act as our anchors for guidance. Without personal anchors we may feel totally lost. Finding our feet again after a storm can be a question of placing and fixing new anchors and of rediscovering and connecting with old anchorage points.

TIPS

- Get to know what your deepest values are. Identify to whom and what you are true.
- Identify the parts of your life that feel right or feel wrong and identify the core causes if you can.
- What symbols and icons surround you to confirm 'who you are'? What do these things say about you and why are the associated messages important to you?
- Honour your self.
- Mentors can be a great help when it comes to looking at fundamental change.
- If you don't have a good mentor, adopt one.
- You may need different mentors and coaches in different dimensions of your life at different times.

Uses

Establishing the foundations of good mental health and of effective living and working. Dealing with change.

Further Reading

See 'Assumption-busting' in the Creativity Tools section. Read also the module on the boundaries of perception, and in particular the module on personal values.

Module 36

Personal Values

We hold in mind a set of values that guide what we will do. You may not be consciously aware of what they are, but they are there.

For example, we tend to feel happy or 'well' when what we are doing or the people we are working with 'fit' with our values. Working according to your values can lead to a sense of fulfilment and happiness. Conversely, we may feel at odds with life and we lose energy when what we are doing does not fit with your values. Clearly, this impacts performance.

Your deepest, most central values are held to be so important that they are wedded to your sense of survival. You become aware of these deepest values when challenged. Any perceived challenge to your 'survival' can trigger the release of a huge amount of 'survival energy': strong emotional reactions and an overwhelming primitive override of rational thinking. This cascade of events can have a profound impact on the way you think and behave.

If you are unaware of your core values, then you are operating in the dark. Knowing what your core values are can light your way forward.

What We See

Some people seem to continue to operate with ease and clarity no matter what they are faced with. They seem to be well 'aligned' with themselves and with their world. In contrast, some of us may feel confused and don't know quite why we are uncomfortable with a situation that other people seem to find acceptable. When we operate in accordance with what we deeply value, we feel right. When we go against what we deeply value, we feel wrong. We all have values, but not everyone has sat down, uncovered and named them.

> Ben Franklin carried inside his pocket watch, a list of
> 13 virtues he chose to live by.

The extent to which we live according to our values will determine the clarity with which we are able to operate. If we go with our values, we are more likely to succeed in what we do. So the first thing we need to know is what our personal core values actually are.

What to Do

Start to write down what is most important to you. Identify what your rules for living are. If you can, verify these with friends. What do they see in your behaviour that suggests your personal priorities?

When someone else breaches one of your deep 'core' values, a very strong feeling is produced. Reflect upon occasions when this happened and consider what values where involved. When a situation felt either very right or very wrong what values were supported or denied? Name and list them.

If you are in a hurry to find out and uncover what you already know deep down, get an industrial psychologist to help you uncover your central values. If you would like a personal value-finding kit, you may order one via the web site **http://www. spreid.com/book**

Why This Is Important

Values are at the heart of who you are and guide your choices and actions. Knowing your core values can be a source of self-confidence: *if we act true to what we believe, we can validate 'who we are'.*

The quality of your life is determined by the extent to which you are able to align your innermost values and beliefs with the world you operate within and with the company you keep. High-performance individuals and teams operate in alignment with what they and their colleagues deeply believe.

> *Higher levels of performance depend upon how well you live in harmony with your core values.*

The ability to operate in accordance with your core values can be the basis of happiness and fulfilment. If you feel unfulfilled, there may be many reasons, but one could involve unrealised, misaligned or challenged values.

TIPS

- Try to identify your top values.
- How do you honour your values?
- What activity confirms these values for you?

Uses

Building self-awareness, confidence, high performance, decision-making ability and a sense of fulfilment.

Next Steps

Get to know and become familiar with your values. When you know their names, reaffirm your values in how you live, in what you do and in what you say.

Last Words

Your core values constitute the essential you. They shape your character, steer the most important decisions you take and guide your behaviour.

Master and live in harmony with your values and you will feel as if you are going with your own flow of energy. The challenges in front of you will still be there but you will be better positioned to face them.

You have a better chance of performing well and of being happy if you can live true to your values and align yourself with other people who operate with similar ones.

Module 37

Higher Self-awareness and Self-confidence

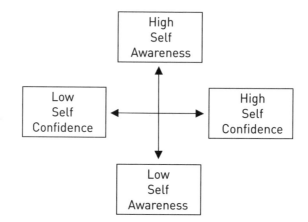

High levels of self-awareness in the absence of a sense of confidence can lead to anxiety. Increasing your performance through higher self-awareness will be undermined if the awareness only serves to undermine your self-confidence. Overcoming and working past doubts and uncertainties will make you stronger and help you perform at a higher level. Self-awareness plus a genuine sense of security, experience and ability are gateway skills to higher performance.

What We See

Increasing your self-awareness will show you parts of yourself you may not be happy or content with. Also, operating within an increasingly vague environment can lead to substantial self-doubt and emotional outbursts.

What to Do

Get to know yourself and your strengths and weaknesses. You will see each strength has a weakness and every weakness a strength. Coming to terms with yourself becomes progressively easier once you know your values, your anchors and how you choose to define yourself.

None of us can be perfect, especially given the passage of time. We are human and will make mistakes. The ability to forgive yourself and others, as well as the ability to begin anew, are also important skills to have.

These modules progressively paint a picture of Territories Two, Three and Four, where eventually there are fewer and fewer hard, crisp, clear answers in life. Self-confidence is required, despite increasing uncertainty.

Self-confidence building requires that you believe in what you are doing, that you believe you are 'safe', and that you have the skills and resources to deliver what you say you will deliver when you said you would. With this in mind, it is always a good idea to keep the promises you make to yourself. It is a good idea to set up positive reaffirming feedback loops that confirm your self-assessments and confidence. This is unlikely to happen if you cannot trust yourself to keep your own promises to yourself.

It goes without saying that you should maintain and constantly extend your professional abilities, as the speed of change means that standing still would result in you moving backwards relative to your peer group.

Your ability to keep up with social trends is an important aspect of building and maintaining a wide range of abilities.

Building self-awareness should go hand in hand with a conscious process of building self-confidence.

TIPS

- **On awareness**: get as many of the more frequently used professionally administered psychometric tests done on yourself as you can stand. Write down your estimates of the results **before** you take the tests then compare these with what you are told.
- **On confidence**: buy a variety of books on building self-confidence and work your way through these.
- Try to estimate where you believe you could be stronger and get some training to build and exercise these weaker mental muscles.

Use

Building self-esteem, confidence in yourself and credibility with others. Must be used authentically.

Overuse

Self-indulgence and distraction.

Decisions

Module 38

Higher Level Decisions and Problems

We are born with a clean slate: an open mind upon which we paint life's big picture. From the moment we have to make a choice, we must make judgements. Some decisions and judgements are simple, but many are not. Our ability to develop choices depends on a variety of influences, such as our current motivation, and our orientation to risk and certainty, plus a multitude of other preferences that we pick up along the way.

This next section aims to prepare us for thinking about and dealing with problems, and how we might use our various thinking skills to take better decisions. In attempting to resolve a problem, few people give consideration to the type of problem they are dealing with **before** they choose a **mental process template** or a course of action.

Know What Type of Problem You Have

It's a good idea to know what you might be dealing with when you face a problem, before choosing what to do. Not all problems allow us the luxury of neat and tidy, logical determination to equally clear-cut, unambiguous decisions.

There are basically two classes of problem.

Class One – Simple, unambiguous and fully open to logic. There may be volume and depth of detail issues, but these will have limits. People with Territory One ability can deal adequately with these.

Class Two – Complex, slippery decisions, of which there are several species. People with Territory Two ability will cope with incomplete issues involving some degree of ambiguity.

In Territory Three, a higher level of ability is required to cope with dilemmas and seemingly separate issues that are actually bound together in some way. These will be dealt with in section three of this book (see modules 62 and 63).

There is one fundamental aspect of our society's prevailing attitude concerning the very idea of a '**problem**' that we should consider first. With this in mind, the next module looks at the problem with problems.

Module 39

The Problem with Problems

In the West, we seem to have a fundamental difficulty with the idea of 'problems' right from the start. Thinking about problems begins with the very word itself. We view 'problems' as bad or unwanted things, and we generally adopt a negative attitude toward them.

For example, when was the last time you said, 'Fantastic – what a great problem!' when things were not going as well as expected.

If we start with the wrong attitude toward a challenge we may limit our performance.

What We See

Eskimos have many different words for snow that quickly characterise local conditions. We only have a few. Likewise, we in the West have a limited choice of words for 'problem'. Look the word up in a thesaurus and all the alternative words are negative. The Japanese, on the other hand, have different, somewhat enlightening descriptions for problems, such as, 'There are those that produce a benefit and those that do not.'

Problems can create a sense of purpose. Having ownership of useful problems to solve can generate a sense of personal relevance and can define who you are. Ironically, many people relish the idea of a problem-free life; however, *when we have no problems at all we risk losing a sense of purpose and may cease to feel relevant; we risk becoming pointless.* Imagine a life of total ease, devoid of challenge – for a while it would be a pleasant rest, but ultimately such a life would feel dull.

Sometimes very successful people or very wealthy individuals can experience severe difficulty with their lives because they have 'arrived' and everything is too easy. There is no stretch, no learning, and no point. Sometimes early success and/or sudden wealth are no blessing. (I'm told there is a club for depressed millionaires).

> *In the absence of problems, would we exist in a state of bliss or eternal numbness? And how would we know the difference?*

Problems can cause discomfort, but some are healthy and provide useful stimuli to stretch our abilities. It is not unusual, therefore, to find people consciously or unconsciously looking for or creating problems. Given that we are born with the ability to think and with free choice, *the problems we choose to take on are important.*

What to Do

Be '**pro-problem**'. Adopt a different view toward interesting and useful problems. An alternative view to Western society's negative perception would be to regard problems as an opportunity to learn or to see a new path, or as a blessing. However, in order to do this, we need to be self-aware, and aware of our context. It would help, perhaps, if we evolved some new words along with new attitudes. '**Pro-problem**' could be one that helps us in some way.

Why This Is Important

A positive frame of mind has been shown to make a big difference when it comes to happiness and successful outcomes in difficult situations. A positive frame of mind helps differentiate champions from the rest. So be 'pro-problem'. Go looking for 'pro-problems'.

TIPS

- Be inspired. Read books and watch recordings on the subject. Meet people who have a strong positive outlook. Find out how they face problems.
- Ignore, be deaf to those who moan, are negative and say, 'You can't, you will never, it's impossible.'
- Choose truly interesting problems – challenges and stretches to your ability and experience.

Uses

As part of a philosophy for personal fulfilment and commercial success.

Module 40

Error and Serendipity

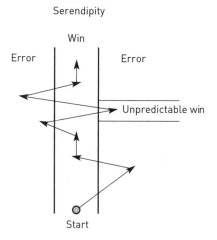

Our performance and behaviour can be shaped by how we 'fit' with one of two fundamental attitudes/behaviour patterns toward error.

- Start early, do something quickly in order to get going. Accept that there will be lots of mistakes and learn as you go.
- Plan everything first and act only when ready (later). Do very little until you are certain, so there are few mistakes, if any.

The first behaviour pattern is more chaotic and involves more risk, but because error tolerance is higher, curiosity concerning interesting 'failures' can lead to a rich flow of alternative discoveries. The second pattern is less error-tolerant and theoretically might involve less risk, but may cut out curiosity and serendipity.

Fear of error can be a big barrier to future performance. Attitude to error significantly affects the way individuals and groups think and behave.

What We See

If you come from a culture that regards mistakes as something to be ashamed of, then your tendency will be to avoid them or cover them up. The project stays on the prescribed rails and you dispose of any errors.

The problem with being ashamed of mistakes is that a rich source of unintended discovery is missed. Serendipity means a 'happy accident' and several have led to breakthrough discoveries. The most often quoted case of serendipity is the British discovery of the life-saving drug Penicillin. This antibiotic has saved millions of lives and opened up the path to the field of antibacterial medicine. Viagra® was another serendipitous discovery. This billion-dollar drug could easily have been rejected because it failed in its original medical trials as a potential heart drug. Curiosity was sparked when vigilant researchers noticed some interesting side effects. It is a mistake not to look with new eyes at our errors.

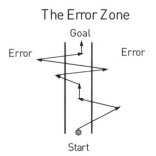

The Error Zone

Of course, some error is error plain and simple. There have been several examples of currency and metal traders creating colossal losses and then racking up even more in attempts to win back their earlier losses. No doubt there will be more in the future.

A young, hard-working executive took a multi million-dollar loss because of an error on a computer contract. As soon as the error became apparent, he decided he would resign rather than wait to be fired. On the next Monday morning he presented his letter to the head of the business, who said, 'Your resignation is not acceptable, we've just spent millions on your education!' Powerful stories last. They travel widely, give permission and set standards of accepted behaviour. You can create your own stories that embed a lasting message.

What to Do

Error needs to be discussed openly and impersonally, as a shared fact of life. Look for what is interesting about the error. What can a particular error teach us? Are there interesting clusters of 'errors' or anomalies?

Promote people who are prepared to make big bets and fail. Manage the culture so that error is dealt with in a positive, non-career threatening and safe way. If we act in teams, then teams should share how errors are positively acknowledged and dealt with.

Again this is a subject that needs to be 'balanced'. On the one hand, there is the need to maintain a procedure or a routine, whilst on the other there is a need to be vigilant for useful anomalies and 'happy accidents'. Too much control and a system becomes rigid; with too little control, people and systems become sloppy.

Why This Is Important

Curiosity and inventive discovery are curtailed if 'error' is seen as a bad thing. A lot of time and energy are wasted in anxious cover up of errors and the avoidance of blame.

Breakthrough discoveries can be missed if serendipity is not allowed.

Checks and balances for error are still required, because some errors WILL sink a business. One of Britain's oldest banks sank spectacularly under a mountain of debt run up by just one currency dealer who tried, unsuccessfully, to cover his mistakes.

I once worked with a big organisation that wanted to cut costs. Some of the engineers ridiculed management's petty-mindedness because they stopped serving biscuits at meetings, saving pennies whilst the engineers' own suggestions could have saved thousands.

At my first meeting, I suggested lavish biscuits as standard – just so that people could laugh at the error and to give the story a legitimacy that would keep people focused on the real goal of saving money in a good way.

Remember, decisions have a scale of impact. Ensure your decisions are commensurate with the situation, or you will be ridiculed and lose support. News of your decisions has a wider symbolic impact than you would imagine. The grapevine is 1,000 times more effective than the internal magazine.

TIPS

- Those areas of the organisation in which error must be stopped and dealt with rapidly must be well signposted, and procedures for recovery well known.
- Learn to laugh when you make a mistake. It improves both your sense of well-being and your ability to learn. Be prepared to share the laughter with others occasionally – it provides relief from tension and permission to change.
- Put error on your management agenda as a positive learning opportunity. Try to make error exposure fun, so that any negative tension can be dissipated in a positive way. The goal is to promote earlier, full disclosure.
- Fix the process, fix the problem, provide help where it is required, and then there is no need to blame. Blame serves no useful purpose in a team. If an error occurs, it is the whole team's responsibility.

Uses

Innovation. New product development. Customer care (by following up and improving something). Quality control and team motivation.

Additional Note Regarding Scale Error

With simple error, we may fail to do the right thing well or at all. Scale error is when we do the right thing, but fail to fully exploit all the available opportunities.

Then there is 'dumb luck': we do the wrong thing, believing we are on the right path, but end up with a much better result than we could have originally hoped for. 'Parallel error', which is covered in the next module, is quite different from 'dumb luck'. With parallel error, the outcome is generally not a good one.

Module 41

Parallel Error

This is a serious perceptual error to which we are all prone.

Parallel error occurs in our decision-making processes when we make information fit the wrong way into something we believe to be true that is actually false.

For example, a cross-country runner friend of mine describes an experience in which he ran energetically to a position way ahead of the pack, having read all the indications and signs properly, but then suddenly realised that a river 'shouldn't be where it now was'. Of course it is ridiculous to believe a river would move its course to confound one runner. When he came to his senses and re-checked his map with an open mind, he discovered he was actually five miles off track! He had shoehorned earlier data to fit a wrong perception. He'd created a 'parallel error' in his mental processing of 'the facts'.

We are at risk in several parts of our social and work lives if we fail to spot parallel error. Organisations can suffer too, if everyone thinks they are on the right track when in fact they have misread the signals and are headed in the wrong direction.

What We See

Orienteering is a high-intensity, competitive sport available to people of all ages. It involves thinking under pressure, map-reading, scanning the terrain for markers, and running, all at the same time.

We can succumb to parallel error in our friendships and our commercial decisions. We read a few of the available signs and make what we actually see fit with what we were expecting or hoping to see. In this manner, we proceed blindly and often at great cost along the wrong path.

Parallel errors in business are easy to see after the fact because they involve a huge about-turn. Microsoft's first decision that 'Netscape and the internet are not a challenge', illustrates a profound misreading of the road map to the future. Microsoft subsequently made a very public about-turn and placed a massive emphasis on the internet. They could afford to make this sort of mistake and correct it. Many smaller outfits would have gone broke and people would have lost their jobs.

What to Do

Regularly check your ideas and your work with other people, especially those who are independent. Ask for and listen openly to the advice people give. Find ways of getting advice and clear cross-referencing in a timely manner when you are under high levels of pressure.

Review your fundamental decisions and what these commit you to, and, importantly, which avenues are closed off as a consequence.

Ask the simple question, what if we have got this wrong? How could these signs and this evidence be seen with fresh eyes and minds?

Why This Is Important

Parallel error works in groups and with individuals. We look foolish when we make this sort of mistake.

TIPS

- If you make this mistake, it is often best to laugh, admit your humanity and backtrack, making doubly sure you are now on track.
- Alarm bells should ring when independent advice tells you the opposite of what you expected. To this end, avoid 'yes men and women'.
- Make sure your checking system includes people who are comfortable with conflict and who are likely to have alternative viewpoints.
- Try triangulating with other people.
- Send people on ahead to check the way before you commit the whole group.

Uses

Error prevention. Avoiding embarrassing events. Avoiding costly backtracks and having to then pay or invest double to get back to where you wanted to be. Judiciously asking, 'Have we got this wrong?' once in a while allows you to maintain and recover credibility.

Feeling and Thinking

Module 42

Emotional/Logical Balance

Many things are balanced. One important balance that should be considered if we wish to have high-performance ability is that between logic and emotion; in other words, between our heads and hearts.

For example, if we allowed our world to be run entirely on a logical basis we'd all turn into cold, dry fish. Our logic is of little use if, lacking human warmth, what we say fails to influence other people. A life lived with an excess of emotion, however, would turn us into hysterical wrecks. Performance is a matter of striking the appropriate balance.

What We See

Our ability to think clearly can, quite literally, be hijacked by emotion. This hijacking process is no accident of nature. Mental hijacking is a vital survival response that is driven by overwhelmingly powerful primordial emotion. The body's priority will always be to survive first, think second.

We need emotion. Without emotion what we offer to other people can seem false, cold or distant, or lacking authenticity as coming from a human being – the gift of a mere robot. At the same time we cannot do without logic because logic sits at the heart of 'sensible' reasoning and scientific development. Happiness and high performance in the end will be a matter of you finding your own appropriate balance between your expression of both rational and emotional influences.

What to Do

We need to find value in our logic as well as the worth of our feelings and emotions. We need to beware overuse of either logic or our emotions. Much of our education system facilitates our rational skills, but for many people there is significantly less opportunity to practise or discuss emotions. In regard to your emotional development:

- When you detect or feel that 'the balance is off' do something about it. Get professional help if necessary. Find people who are competent in balancing logic and emotion.
- Some people keep deeply personal diaries in which they bring what they feel to the fore, not for the sake of sharing the feelings but to give the feeling 'voice'. Acknowledging the presence of a feeling is important. Once a feeling has a name you can do something about it.
- Give a feeling voice by telling someone how you feel. This does not require the other person to do anything but may make you feel better knowing the feeling is now OUT instead of bottled up INSIDE you.
- Mental constipation is just as bad as physical constipation. Both are painful, both will out in the end and remedies for both require discretion.

Why This Is Important

Happiness and performance depend upon how well we balance the rational and the emotional aspects of our lives.

TIP

- Only involve people you trust and with whom you feel secure in any development of your emotions.

Use

To re-balance our lifestyle and relationships with other people.

Next Steps

Ask one or two close friends if they think you have the best balance for you between being serious and logical and being in touch with your feelings. What do they suggest in the way of beneficial changes?

Last Words

Where we strike our personal balance is very much a matter of personal preference. There is no such thing as a perfect balance. A balance will only be perfect for a while; as the world rotates, things change and the balance will have to be adjusted. Life is dynamic: it is why we are here and why we cannot stay.

Module 43

Doing the Splits: Ambiguity and Tension

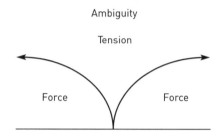

In life, we are often pulled by opposing forces. We are asked to make decisions or to take action that somehow has to balance two competing needs. If we as individuals or as groups get the emphasis wrong in our decisions and actions, then our performance will suffer. The pull of two opposing forces creates a strong sense of ambiguity and in some people a sense of 'tension'. An ability to manage sensations of tension and ambiguity is important if you wish to perform at higher levels.

By way of example, imagine you are in control of your own company. On the one hand you may want to spend more money investing in increasing future sales BUT you may also want to cut spending to increase profits now.

We can visualise the major forces at work within an ambiguity as pulling in opposite directions, as illustrated above. Coping with such opposing forces is a matter of being able to mentally practise what gymnasts call 'doing the splits'. Imagery of 'the splits' can help us to visualise where the balance is being struck within a tension. Like all good gymnasts we need to mentally flex our thinking, our attitudes and our behaviour in order to acquire this particular skill.

What We See

At work and at home we are pulled in different directions. We are increasingly asked to balance conflicting priorities with multiple demands upon limited resources of time, assets and attention. Often these forces operate in opposition and create tension.

Trying to do what gymnasts call 'the splits' is painful but possible with a lot of training and exercise. As our legs head off in opposite directions, a gymnast's exercises aim to stretch normally taut sinews to go that bit further. Mentally doing the splits when dealing with an ambiguity is therefore a matter of exercise and tolerance. A few people can physically do 'the splits' but the rest of us quickly discover an early pain barrier that stops us hurting ourselves.

> *Think of the tension caused by ambiguity using this analogy: Imagine some-one is required to run between two fixed points. Around the runner's waist are tied two elastic cords that are also anchored at two fixed points, say 100 metres apart. As our runner runs in any direction there will be a proportionate force pulling him back to one or both of the fixed points. There may well be a point at which tension is lowest for our runner. However, if the point of lowest tension happens to be 'a swamp full of alligators' then the only way to get to a desired place, given the constraints, is to put in the effort and live with the tension.*

Work Tensions

Tensions can arise at work where the desires expressed by conversations A clash with B at any level.

Conversations A	Conversations B
Control	Experiment
Cut costs	Invest and spend more money
Just in time	New product development
Process re-engineering	New business development
Total quality management	Research and development
Avoid risk	Let's try something new
Financial engineering	Building a business
Tight budgets	Dreams and visions
Focus on now	Focus on the future

There is no such thing as a formula for success for dealing with contradictory forces within employment institutions and within relationships. It is entirely possible to be successful with different levels of emphasis on differing priorities at different times.

Personal Life Tensions

Conversations A	Conversations B
Time at home	Time developing a career
Time with partner	Time with children
Money for 'now'	Money for 'later'
Being sensible	Having some fun
Free time	Work
Having	Being
Individual needs	Fitting in
Change and novelty	Predictability, steadiness

People and organisations that remain successful for longer are likely to be those that are best able to manage their contradictions well. Where conversations are equally entertained from A and B (see above) there is increased scope for challenge and counter-challenge. The good aspect of this challenge is it keeps systems and people on their toes; evolution is encouraged in our personal lives and at work. Absolute systems may well succeed briefly; however, those that are dynamic tend to prevail in the longer term.

More on What We See

Within work and family life, these tensions are very real. Careers and personal relationships are built and dashed depending on how well people manage these tensions. People in organisations holding powerful positions of authority do get passionate about their beliefs and will fight off equally passionate people who uphold an opposing view. Both sides believe that they alone have the one correct answer.

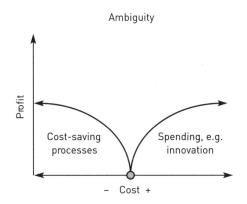

At the higher levels of thinking ability we will see how there are situations in which the success of the whole depends on BOTH opposing views being held as valid at the same time despite the contradictions. Nullifying one debilitates the other. (See polarities and multarities).

> *Life is not pure, nor absolute.*
> *Attempts to force a dynamic system to be 'pure and simple'*
> *are naïve and can be extremely destructive or cruel.*

Sometimes a feeling or a tension within an ambiguity is what actually provides a situation with energy or life. Taking away tension can literally kill off something valuable.

> *In essence a sense of contest created by an ambiguity*
> ***should not be one to win but one to balance.***

The contest should therefore be within you as much as it is with others.

Modules 44 to 46 Sub-optimal Tension Maps

Module 44

Breakage

We can sketch several simple maps of such forces at work, making it easy to predict a variety of outcomes. These tension maps can be just as easily re-interpreted for personal relationships.

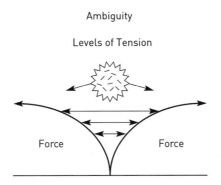

Ambiguity

Levels of Tension

Force   Force

How Much Is Too Much?

People as well as institutions have their tolerance levels for tension. If there is too much tension, damage occurs. People and organisations therefore adopt self-defence mechanisms. Some defence mechanisms will be clear and explicit whilst others may be hidden, subtle or tacit.

Module 45

Dominance

The trick is to place and maintain effective limits to keep tension high enough to be interesting and useful, but not so high that damage occurs. Sometimes the balance can slip, as the illustration below suggests.

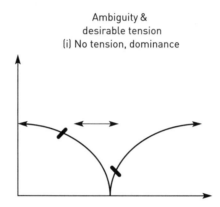

Ambiguity &
desirable tension
(i) No tension, dominance

In this case, tension forces may well have been identified and limits put in place, but one side has pulled too far and dominated the other. This side has won, but the relationship or the organisation may have lost as a result. In this situation the opposing forces or personalities are not equally matched or controlled to produce an optimal balance.

When one force/person/department/organisation is totally dominated by the other there is no fiery productive energising tension. A dictator may have won control but will have lost his nation. The power of ambiguity has been lost. Life is simpler but altogether much less rich.

When just one side dominates, the pattern remains the same. There will be a narrow-sighted sense of clarity, little or no vision and poor motivation. This can also happen within us too. Head and heart need balance.

Module 46

Stalemate

The chart below is an illustration of a situation in which the two opposing forces are either too constrained or perhaps too polite to develop real tension. Again life is relatively simple and unchallenged here. There may be a sense of futile frustration or a sense of resignation or even peculiar forms of game-playing to avoid tension.

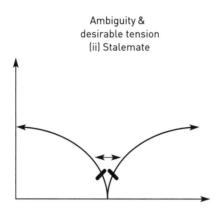

Ambiguity &
desirable tension
(ii) Stalemate

Essentially this is a flaccid situation. There is no power, no sense of tension. The edicts and words are there but the power to move has been muted. Inspiration happens only outside of the relationship or the organisation.

What to Do

In doing the splits a little pain is necessary in order to know where the current limits are. Stretch is required to get up to and beyond those limits if we wish to grow.

When we get lazy or when we fail to grow, we can end up feeling lifeless and without the vitality of our youth. This can happen when we are faced with increasingly familiar difficulties that become easier to deal with either at home or at work.

Sometimes a new problem, a change or a new adventure with new uncertainties can be a blessing.

A desirable situation is to be in a position of matched contradictions, in which the outer AND the inner limits are known and maintained. Too little tension can be as bad as too much. The important thing is to strike a good balance.

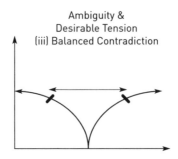

Ambiguity &
Desirable Tension
(iii) Balanced Contradiction

A balance cannot be struck if everyone thinks of the situation in terms of absolutes. So when attempting to deal with an ambiguous situation it is a good idea to ditch the value of 'absolutes'. Get used to the word 'sometimes' as opposed to 'always'. Often the better 'deals' or outcomes involve higher levels of tension. A judgement as to what other people can tolerate is necessary.

> *Every wave needs a rock to splash upon to prove itself a wave.*
> *If you are that rock, where is your wave?*

The key to dealing effectively with ambiguity is not to attempt to drive it out of the system but to accept that there will always be tension in the workplace and in our personal lives. If we remain self-aware we can learn to harness the energy generated by an ambiguity to good effect.

Try to picture who or what is pulling in what direction. Consider the drive or motivation for each direction in which you are being pulled or pushed. What is being valued and why? Try to get to know what the contradictions are and accommodate what you can. The trick is to get the most for everyone AND to live with some heightened sense of tension. Fighting off or dealing with the feelings generated by one of our instincts may also be part of the equation.

Remember that an ambiguous situation is not always one that can be resolved; often it must be accommodated: 'lived with'. Therefore the ability to compromise and adapt are essential skills.

TIPS

- If the whole issue can be rendered simple it can often be easier to deal with. In dealing with such complexity, absolute influence and pure outcomes will be rare.
- Sometimes there may be a smaller number of pivotal issues that exert disproportionate influence.

- Rather than deal with all the dimensions, look for leverage points at the nexus or within pivotal issues. When faced with a muddle of complex issues, one approach is to try to find the origin, the nexus or the focal points within the complexity.

- Once you accept that the outcomes may be partial, a resolution may be easier to find.

Uses

These maps can help us visualise and deal with everyday home and work life. Many aspects of our lives involve ambiguity.

Relationships and Reality

Module 47

Three Realities: Reid's Reality Funnel

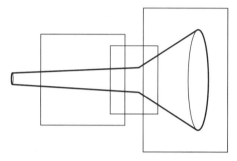

Knowing where your personal perception pattern sits relative to other people is important. There are at least three fundamentally different priorities for the ways of thinking when it comes to certainty and tolerance of ambiguity. It is easy to clash with people who have a different profile, and performance can fall. Performance can be improved by understanding the differences.

For example, someone who lives and breathes detail and clear unambiguous rules and procedures will probably clash quite badly with someone who accomplishes things without detail or procedure.

Reid's Perception Funnel is produced when we combine the certainty funnel with frames of reference to describe how different people might think. This model creates three 'worlds' in which people might choose to operate. Loose, weak boundaries sit on the right, while tight, high-definition boundaries sit on the left. These two are bridged by a third, moderately ambiguous world.

What We See

This results in a simple yet practical map that may illuminate three alternative perceptions of reality. Our perception shapes the way we think. Since what we think shapes behaviour, this map can indicate how different people might express quite different ways of dealing with the world – as they see it. The general shape of the funnel may change but the three generalised 'worlds' remain.

The central drivers in this model are tolerance of uncertainty together with our individual tendency to live and behave according to our preferences. Whilst we all possess a variety of abilities, many of us will tend to operate using the skills we prefer in situations in which we feel most comfortable. In other words, we will generally gravitate toward situations and job, life and partnership roles that support our personal preferences.

In life as in work, each person's frame will have quite different boundaries beyond which he as an individual will not be comfortable. Where we are able to, we tend to move away from discomfort and toward comfort. We tend to exercise our preferences and seek situations that are either familiar or in which we feel safe, competent, productive or happy. We can only comfortably 'flex' what we do as far as our abilities and tolerance will allow us.

Remember the following notes are generalisations – a partial truth and an approximate indicator. Different people will travel different distances along these territories.

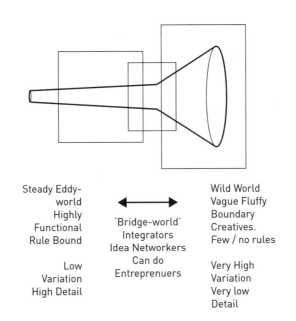

| Steady Eddy-world
Highly
Functional
Rule Bound | ◄────►
'Bridge-world'
Integrators
Idea Networkers
Can do
Entreprenuers | Wild World
Vague Fluffy
Boundary
Creatives.
Few / no rules |
| Low
Variation
High Detail | | Very High
Variation
Very low
Detail |

Left-hand Realm: Steady Eddy World

Appeals to anyone who loves lots of detail, and clear rules and procedures – 'everyday troopers'. My favourite description here is of 'Steady Eddy' (Edwina or Edward). In Steady Eddy World the general frame of reference has a high level of certainty. Life is relatively predictable and people follow and obey clear rules. Causes and effects are squarely linked. In this world high levels of detail are possible because uncertainties are perceived to be rare.

Bridge World: Integrators (The Ambiguity Bridge)

A place between logic and the chaotic cauldron of emerging realities. This place is given over to moderate to high levels of ambiguity. People here are often good 'integrators' and great leaders. Integrators are great at making lots of useful connections between people and ideas. They are really good at making practical sense out of vague fluffy ideas, but they are rarely 'completer/finishers'. Leaders operating with this style will be visible and viable, whereas other middle management integrators may be less well appreciated or may be seen as an indulgence and will therefore be vulnerable during a recession.

Right-hand Realm: Wild World

This environment and the people in it are almost the opposite of Steady Eddy World – this area attracts freelance people who hate boundaries. Visionaries, writers and strategists, artists and quite a few politicians live here. In Wild World 'normal' rules do not apply, nor should they be expected to. Detail cannot persist in Wild World because it is volatile and rules don't last very long, if at all. In Wild World there is an attraction toward uncertainty, risk and novelty.

Consider two different people. One adopts the preferences of and lives predominantly within the narrow well-bounded confines of the left-hand side of the funnel; whilst the other prefers to operate mostly on the looser open end shown on the right. Each person adopts the attitudes and behaviours that coincide with his orientation to certainty. On the left there is a preference for predictability, reason and hard logic; whilst on the right the preference is for high uncertainty, novelty and change.

Who Does What and Why?

The distribution of different types of people with their particular orientations toward certainty, risk and novelty will vary between families and organisations. The generally long funnel illustrated above might represent an organisation facing a long period of stability, whereas below we might interpret this alternative map as a family or organisation that is ready for rapid change and high levels of uncertainty.

For example, an expatriate career family that can move house and country at the drop of a hat might fit this shorter funnel model. At an organisational level, notice the difference in the numbers of people needed in each realm and the likely style and balance of decision-making indicated by quite different patterns. Bringing together different patterns could cause intractable problems: for example, in a merger or acquisition. The same transition difficulties arise if the wider climate alters to be faster or slower paced.

There will also be a marked difference in the way each of these two people deal with and tolerate 'risk'. Whilst the two extremes are relatively easier to describe, someone who lives in the transition zone presents difficulties since he has the characteristics of a chameleon. This type of person bridges the two worlds, having one foot in the realm of reasoned hard logic on the left and the other in the highly volatile territory on the right.

What to Do

- Compare and contrast the lifestyles, aspirations and behaviours of the people you work with and the ones you work for. Map them out.
- Make sure you shape your delivery according to their senses of reality. This applies to your family, customers, boss, etc.
- Consider what is required and whether or not your presentation is broad-brush or high-detail.
- Use the language that fits the realm you are addressing.
- If you need to communicate with people from different realms use language and methods appropriate to their 'worlds', their realities, their realms.
- Consider the strategic implications of the population of people you are dealing with relative to the rate and pace of change of their context. You might wrongly believe that you are 'out there' because you once were; but are you now? Check out the view of the world held by today's 18-year-olds. How does this compare to what you AND your present peer group think?

Why This Is Important

Reid's Reality Funnel is a very useful way of describing the boundaries we create and how these are related to what we believe we need and want. As we go through life we seek to confirm and validate our own particular view of what we believe reality is.

The downside of channelling our perception to fit our view of reality is that we may dismiss an equally valid, better alternative view of reality as unreasonable. Clearly if we are wrong, channelled and self-limited in some way, this will impact performance.

Given the gradient within the perception funnel, opinions will differ considerably. This can become the fuel of either creative or destructive conflict. People will uphold (often by fighting for) their personal individual boundaries and will believe they are being entirely reasonable in doing so.

TIPS

- Know your orientation on the funnel and ally yourself to people who are comfortable in the other two areas.

- How does your life partner operate within this model and how do you compare with each other? Have opposites attracted or are you similar?

- How do you 'fit' into the wider scheme of things?

- Do you fit the profile of the industry or the organisation you are in?

- Has your appetite for certainty changed over time? If so, what will you do next? Take care to avoid illusion.

- One way of dealing with change is to work carefully on peoples' perceptions well in advance of what is planned.

Uses

In understanding how you might best communicate with people who see the world from a different perspective than your own. Use to understand and create alternative points of view during a negotiation or conflict or in an attempt to influence someone.

Next Steps

Reflect upon the people you know – where do they 'live' within this model? Consider how you might authentically communicate with them using their concepts of reality as your guide.

Further Reading

See section on uncertainty and strategic planning. See later modules on perception.

Beloit College in Wisconsin, USA, produces an informative insight into the shared mindset of current 18-year-olds: **http://www.beloit.edu**. Click on the link 'only@ Beloit' or search for 'mindset'.

Winning Philosophies

Module 48

How Do You Define Yourself?

How we define ourselves impacts the way we think and behave. We invest a perception of value and focus energy toward maintaining the definition of who we believe we are and what we think we stand 'for'. Sometimes these definitions of who we believe we are can become badly positioned, out of date, incomplete or just wrong.

If you are **defined by the problems you adopt** then consider what role 'stretch' has in your philosophy for personal fulfilment. Do you always choose the same sort of problems? If so, why? We all need a balanced amount of stretch. Stretch keeps us aware and alive. Too much stretch and we become ill. Too little and we become listless. The amount of stretch you need at different times will vary considerably, so always aiming to be the best may be unwise. Sometimes its wise to take a break, do nothing and let others win. Again, self-awareness is essential.

For people who are mission- and purpose-minded, there can be a crushing sense of emptiness when they 'arrive'. A strong sense of purpose, aspiration and hope, and the camaraderie of the journey are all closed down upon arrival. There is a genuine sense of loss. Therefore, it is wise to have available to us a new stretch goal that will come into play AFTER we have been successful with our current main mission. Get the new stretch goal or project ready BEFORE you 'arrive'. If it is better to travel in hope than to arrive, always keep in mind the next journey. Will your next journey be a repetition or something really new?

Defined by Money

I once met a woman on a marketing workshop who quickly became distressed and cried when she said that she had recently 'lost' 80% of the budget of which she had been in control. Apparently this money was too important to her. She defined herself, her success and her perception of her status with a particular sum of money. Her management had asked her to do a slightly different sort of work and held her in good regard, yet she was distraught. I asked, 'Are you defining who you are based on this money then?' When she thought how silly that definition of self-worth was, she quickly recovered her composure. She was then able to give all her energy to the job in hand instead of allowing her personal energy to drain away down an imagined black hole.

Letting Go

Each of us has a number of 'vital' issues, perhaps involving people, places, resources or things that we believe really define who we are. We strongly identify with them. Rising to a higher level of mental ability involves being able to interrogate these beliefs and when necessary being able to surrender many of these 'definitions' as actually not important and not really required.

You are who you are, now.

So how do you define yourself? Look at what would upset you the most if you suddenly lost something. Then consider why you hold this to be so important. Ask yourself: are there another ways of framing the importance of the thing that you believe defines who you are?

Because we operate from within a safe frame of reference, a lot of life is an illusion. Self-awareness helps us to see more clearly where we really are, now.

See module 35 on personal anchors. Sometimes it is a good idea to hold fast to some aspects of life that we value until we have alternative anchors available to us.

Territory Three

Hills of Shale, Thick Fog and Swamps
High Uncertainty

Performance and Upgrade

In Territory Two we gained some ability to deal with ambiguity. We learned that issues are often relative as opposed to absolute. We built up a moderate level of tolerance for uncertainty and ambiguity.

What differentiates Territory Three from Territory Two is the ability to hold two competing ideas in mind as valid at the same time. This requires a form of **mental multi-tasking ability** and even **higher levels of tolerance for uncertainty**. Throughout Territory Three you may notice that issues are seen as interconnected, often within inseparable pairs, dualities, dilemmas and contradictions.

An ability to deal with a **duality** is essential when thinking at this level of complexity.

Increased awareness of self and context is apparent at this level of ability, as is **a higher level of emotional skill and sensitivity**.

The key, therefore, in dealing with high levels of ambiguity is in understanding the rules and in deciding how you choose to think and behave *before* you begin. In this section you will find a variety of tools to help you to move from reasonably solid ground through foggy, ambiguous territory.

Upgrade Your Models and Tools

Module 49

Ambiguity Guidelines

There are several reasons for which we experience ambiguity. There is usually a lack of certainty and there are opposing forces that contest for supremacy. Sometimes an ambiguity can be resolved by simply providing missing information and raising the sense of certainty. One side can 'win' absolutely and the situation becomes clear and unambiguous.

Duality Present: Ambiguity Guaranteed

In many situations, however, reaching clarity is never achievable because the structure of the issue involves irrevocable linkages: one issue is firmly bound to the other, there is a duality or some form of dilemma and neither side will allow a clear resolution.

No matter which mental tool or model you choose to employ when dealing with an ambiguity, it is a good idea to reflect on some general guidelines. With high levels of ambiguity you may encounter:

- a lack of clarity
- uncertainties and partial truths
- the absence of absolutes
- alternative, equally plausible interpretations, politics and political manoeuvring
- information that is fluid and may be forming and decomposing at the same time
- missing information, which when found makes no material difference
- contradictions
- a situation that refuses to condense into certainties
- people, issues and forces pulling in opposing directions
- things that change with time, but remain ambiguous
- a whole that remains fluid and dynamic

All of these characteristics defy the basic premise of logic that action and reaction always follow a particular sequence, irrespective of the passage of time. Logic says what is true now remains true tomorrow. **This is not the case with ambiguity**. What is true now may not be true tomorrow. Your ally today could be your enemy tomorrow, and therefore logical reasoning alone cannot help with ambiguity.

Feelings: An Emotional Note

Before we look at specific tips and tools there is one very important point of which we should remind ourselves. When we are faced with an ambiguity our frame of reference is to some extent held 'open'. Because we cannot achieve closure, we experience an increasing sense of uncertainty, and feelings of tension and unease. Living with uncertainty means we have to learn to tolerate 'an open wound' – **and** uncomfortable feelings. A desire to get rid of these awkward feelings can lead us to make poor, premature decisions.

As you move away from the dominant role of cool calm logic, you will notice an increasing role for your emotions. This is especially true in ambiguous, uncertain environments where decisions need to be taken quickly. As you continue to develop increasingly complex, faster ways of living and working, you will discover that your emotions have a valuable role. Fast decision-making involves intuition; in other words, sense- making through your instincts and feelings.

Emotions have a legitimate place in foggy ambiguous landscapes.

Closure is not possible, so 'tension' is always present. Feelings created can be enjoyed or suffered; you might have a choice over which way you feel if you are blessed with a sense of humour.

Tools That May Help

- imagery as anchor points in the mind
- a reliance on relatively crude sensations: intuition, instinct, gut feelings
- decisions based on tilt or balance points combined with feelings
- decisions based on optimum positions and managed secondary positions
- placing bets – a gamble
- discretion, balance and humanity
- philosophy and self-forgiveness

Mental Processing and Performance Patterns

- more than one thought process running at the same time
- high awareness of self and context
- being quick-witted

Results of Decisions

- Only incomplete outcomes are possible – seeking perfect solutions is a recipe for high anxiety.
- Compromise will be involved.

- People will be required to adapt.
- You will be partially correct AND partially wrong at the same time. Not everyone will appreciate this. Since you will not be able to please, or serve, all of the people all of the time, decisions will be political.
- Solutions will be temporary and subject to change.
- Decisions will not always be reproducible and may seem illogical and out of context.

Operating Philosophy

You must find and abide by your own performance philosophy. By degree, a sense of heaven and hell operate side by side here. (Your sanity may be tested.) A few people are sometimes obliged to take highly ambiguous decisions so that the many can live simple unambiguous lives.

Module 50

Simple Solutions to Complex Problems: The Gordian Knot

Some problems look huge, complex and knotty. Occasionally a simple but brutal solution works.

The 'Gordian knot' was a huge rope knot presented as a challenge to Alexander the Great. The oracles of the time had said, 'He who would untie the knot would conquer Asia.' The knot was so complex that it would have been extremely difficult to untie. Rather than struggle, Alexander simply chose to use one mighty swing of his sword to cleave the knot apart.

What We See

Life can present us with all sorts of problems. Other people and the problem itself may suggest that an equally complicated solution may be required. Occasionally, brute force and a sharp instrument will do the job in a simple way.

> *Sometimes a crude solution may be the best approach to complex, knotty problems – that is, of course, if you do **not** value the rope.*

What to Do

There are occasions when, despite what I have already said, a simple solution or brute force is exactly what is needed. Being 'bull-headed' sometimes pays off, but not always.

- Consider all your options before you act.
- Do not rule out the simple solution when faced with something complicated. Complexity may sometimes be more of a case of an error of perception.
- There are a limited number of times a simple but brutal solution can be used in reality.

TIPS

- Cutting to the heart of the matter requires several different strengths. Strength of honest clear perception to see the issues as they really are; mental strength to make the decision; physical and mental energy to follow through and act; and more strength again to live through and deal with the consequences. You need to be of strong character to cut to the quick.
- Have a plan in place to cope with any aftermath.
- This is one of many tools. Just because you are capable of using this solution does not mean you should. In an ideal world you should be in a position in which you have choices over how you will act, according to circumstances.

Uses

Requires discretion. Use only when you have sufficient force and breaking the deadlock is the objective, AND when the knot itself is no longer of value. Useful where speed or a display of will and force is required.

Overuse

You may be regarded as unnecessarily brutal, possibly cruel, and insensitive. People may fear you. Performance may initially rise, only to then fall and retrench at lower levels.

Further Reading

For more on Alexander the Great, read the first section in *The Mask of Command*, by John Keegan, published by Pimlico.

Module 51

Duality and Yin/Yang

Yin and Yang

When dealing with high levels of complexity and/or ambiguous situations, you will notice that issues are often found as inseparable pairs.

Often issues are coupled as opposites. For example, advantage comes with disadvantage. Every strength carries a weakness and at the same time every weakness carries within it a strength. It's a duality.

What We See

The yin/yang image is an ancient and most useful aid for thinking about ambiguity. It shows us that two equal and opposing major forces are constantly at work: bound together in one realm, intimately connected and inseparable. Neither of the two major forces can be cancelled out.

Within yin/yang we see that each force contains an element (the spots) from the other. Many of our attempts to solicit clear absolute outcomes are frustrated by this coupling. It is futile to fight this coupling. Better to understand and accommodate it, as the yin and yang elements are inseparable parts of a whole.

When we look at the whole, we see that many of the interesting aspects of reality are arranged in an unclear, incomplete yet connected and intermingled way.

Statements that fit a yin/yang model would be the idea that, 'In times of peace prepare for war and in times of war prepare for peace.' Or, 'One person's 'dream' is another's nightmare.' One of my favourites is, 'An optimist says he believes we are living in the best of all possible worlds and a pessimist replies that he fears the optimist may be correct.' The yin/yang image has been around for many thousands of years and will endure because this image intelligently conveys so much complexity in one relatively simple picture.

> *Mexican Aztec beliefs held that life and death go hand in hand. There is no 'up' or 'down', no separation of heaven and hell: the Aztecs believed these existed side by side, right now, here on earth. Life gives way to death and death creates an opportunity for life. For them the union of yin and yang represented the wheel of life, relentless, ever turning. Mexican artist Frida Kahlo is seen holding a yin/yang image in one of her may self-portraits. Her identification with the yin/yang representation of the duality in life is not so surprising given her extremely complex life. Remember, this is an ancient Chinese representation of reality that has travelled through and been adopted by different societies on different continents over many thousands of years. As a tool of the mind it has immense value.*

Ambiguities can involve contradictions that may be bound together. When dealing with ambiguity a yin/yang image is especially useful because it can show us that incomplete, i.e., **optimum positions are the most likely outcome**. Also, see how yin/yang might be used in decision-making, in module 62.

What to Do

Picture the issue as two opposing positions. One sits within black whilst the other, interconnected as it is, sits within white.

Some of the rules within yin/yang and with ambiguity are:

- Absolute 100% outcomes are just not possible.
- The system rotates as situations change; advantages become their opposites. Solutions become problematic.
- Partial outcomes are possible, for a while.
- The answer is often 'it depends' – usually on a wider context and an understanding of the prevailing forces at work.
- Making the situation bigger or smaller does not change the basic pattern.
- Even when you have located a broadly acceptable situation it will contain within it a strong element of the opposite.
- All decisions are temporary compromises that will need to be changed and amended as the need arises.
- The goal is never to beat the opposing force because that is never possible. Accommodation and compromise are necessary.

TIPS

- 'Your greatest strength is also your greatest weakness.' It is a mistake to regard strength and weakness as separate issues; they are connected.
- If you are faced with a disadvantage there will be an advantage within the situation. You may not necessarily be in the best position to exploit it, but the new advantage is there never the less.

Uses

Many and varied, in making sense of ambiguous or political situations.

Further Reading

Look out for the symbol in works of art and in other societies. Bound pairs, the philosophy of the 'two-edged sword' and the ideas within Polarity Management™ share common ground.

Module 52

Tracking Multiple Waves

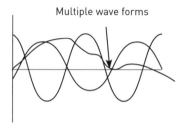

Multiple wave forms

If you are dealing with complex issues, there are usually several issues that require your active attention *at the same time.*

There are many rhythms at work upon us and within us. Some will have a regular shape, but many will not.

It is possible to create an indicative map of how these forces can have a combined impact that might have otherwise not been foreseen.

What We See

Understanding Multiple Waves

The complexity of the path of our lives might be seen as a tangled web, too difficult to look at. Many of the forces that we experience in our lives do have a pattern. We can chart these patterns using short-wave and long-wave imagery, and once we understand the true patterns we can begin to take control.

It is important to have some sort of big picture in mind for work and our personal life. Some people's big picture is all fog. Others might see a collage of imagery, whilst some may see lists of words and routines. Some people may see a variety of models of the world.

One simple place to start is to create an overlapping series of the major trends and influences that act upon us. By understanding our own patterns, we can begin to see how and when life might be easier or tougher. We can see high and low points and therefore better prepare ourselves to choose how and when to react.

What to Do

Individual wave forms or patterns do not tell us very much in isolation. Not inspecting the pattern of our lives isn't helpful. Taking a close look isn't helpful either because a close look may only highlight how tangled and complex things seem to be. We need to see the pattern of our lives from a distance in order to appreciate where the bold strokes are, to see what the general shape is — to appreciate our own place within the big picture. Then we can zoom in and out on the detail of the pattern of our lives in the past, and the most likely future.

The trick is to map several important trends or patterns on the same timescale. Then we can see what the composite picture is. We can see the high and low points in our lives, our relationships, our work or our businesses.

- First identify the forces in operation.
- Map them together. Map them all out on one large chart to show how they interact, overlap, rise and fall.
- Throw in major life or work/life change points and see what coincides.
- Choose the most important forces and map these in different combinations.

Looking at events in isolation distracts from the big picture and can undermine the quality of your thinking. We might make the mistake of believing we are 'unlucky' or helpless victims of circumstance, with no ability to foresee or control events. In many situations, that sort of thinking is plain wrong.

> *If we live only from moment to moment we may enjoy
> summer but freeze in winter.*

We need to step back and see what rises and falls before us.

When we discover what forces are acting upon us we might end up with a graph such as the composite wave illustrated above. Note that all three trends take a dive below the line at one point. This might seem like a period of hard luck at the time, but if you know it's coming you can get ready for the tough time and ride it out. Perceptions of personal pressure can be forestalled. Self-esteem can be maintained.

The example below approximates how a variety of events or forces combine to help or hinder us. This format works just as much in the workplace as it does in your personal life. It can be a crude measuring stick, but a map such as this will alert you to major weak points or opportunities in the future.

Imagine this set of curves and trends is something important to do with your life — how will you interpret its messages?

Multiple wave forms

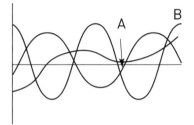

TIPS

- Look for pinch points such as 'A' where the trends all dive toward one low point. At this point, you or your colleagues will be severely tested. This signals a need to be mentally, physically and financially fit enough to weather a predicted storm.

- Look for the opposite, where several trends work collectively in your favour, as in 'B'. Get all the things done that need doing before the next turn down. This is a time to make hay. This is a time to repay and to offer favours, because you can afford to be generous. This is not a time to be arrogant.

- In this model all the lines are flowing in a particular direction. Watch out and beware when the trends widen and 'the scissors open' – you may be overstretching yourself and other people. (See module 32.)

Timescales may be approximate. The aim is to estimate approximately when the good and the bad times are likely to occur in our lives.

Why This Is Important

This model has many applications at home and at work. We start work, progress, retire; our children grow up and go to college, sometimes they return; we get married and get divorced; we are made redundant, and take retraining; our bodies change, our energy and hormonal levels fluctuate; parents get ill and die; job success ebbs and flows.

There are certain trends that affect us all. For example, your personal energy is likely to be higher at age 30 than 50. We are more at risk as we age. Financial earning growth peaks at a given point and starts to fall as we grow older. Our living costs go up and down dramatically. Given just the inevitable aspects of life's wheel, how will these and other trends impact us and importantly – when?

In business, new technologies appear, whole industries are moved wholesale to lower-cost countries, new competitors emerge, profit margins typically get eroded, employee availability and cooperation changes, government intervention changes, staff grow older as do customers, the price of fuel and assets goes up and down, things that were plentiful become scarce, high-value items become generic commodities and a phoenix may rise from its own ashes, re-invigorated despite what the pundits said. Then there are those pesky discontinuous changes that throw the whole apple-cart over, and all the rules change completely. Looking back, they are easy to see in retrospect, but few did.

Uses

As part of a strategic business or life-planning process. Dealing with pending change.

Further Reading

Copies of a personal and a business exercise are available via the web site: **http://www.spreid.com/book**

See cautionary module 32.

Module 53

Mental Multi-tasking: How to Stay 'Open'

(Use 'Bubble Logic')

Ambiguity and bubble thinking

Some people are capable of maintaining two opposing possibilities as separate and viable, where others cannot. They appear to do this by holding their alternative beliefs within what for them are valid but quite separate worlds. If these realities were to be brought into close contact, they could not remain viable.

At one end of the scale we witness healthy people holding on to separate, difficult or desirable realities. At the other end of the scale we may encounter inveterate liars and confidence tricksters. Somewhere in between we see seemingly quite normal people who, when their inhibitions are reduced, let loose a completely different character. The type of person I'm referring to, though, is able to maintain and at will to consciously control these alternative, separate realities.

Some people seem to have a mental strategy whereby they hold contrasting realities within quite separate worlds. Perhaps they do this in order to stay sane, to get what they want or in order to deceive. Their separate worlds are discrete clusters of reasoning, validations and beliefs, each contained within separate 'bubbles' or 'domains'. I call this **'bubble logic'**.

What We See

'**Bubble logic**' is my way of describing how some people seem to be able to accommodate two opposing ideas. Bubble logic is slippery because only parts of the reasoning are sustainable, and other parts are not. Bubble logic is my visualisation of how highly contradictory ideas are managed. People who are capable of using this quite slippery logic are almost entirely credible and seemingly authentic when operating in each of their separate 'worlds'.

Complicated love affairs can involve this sort of separation. One or more players may be able to hold separate realities in which they and their lovers live, because that is what they want and because they are perfectly capable of living this way. For other people who are embroiled in such complications and who do not have the ability to create and maintain such separate worlds, they ultimately become victims of a game they are unable to play.

Really great actors and spies must also be able to divide out their realities and convincingly 'live' the parts they play. Senior people who have to take difficult and hard-edged decisions at work need to be able to switch from their assertive, wilful roles at work to return home as kind, authentic loving life partners and parents to their children.

A situation involving slippery logic may be maintained for good or bad reasons.

Multiple-domains Thinking Skills

My girlfriend and I were having a really blazing hot argument. We were both intensely upset, when the phone rang. My male mind remained locked and focused on the argument, but she paused to answer the telephone. To my amazement, her whole attitude shifted by a quantum step as she pleasantly acknowledged one of her women friends, promised to call her back, hung up the telephone all sweetness and light, and then – boom! We were back into the argument again!

This sequence repeated itself a few years later with another girlfriend. I had stumbled upon a distinct ability. It is as if some people are able to slip between two different realities and engage quite different rules, emotions and thoughts in each place. This is not simply a question of 'rising above' a situation. Clearly this is a useful mental skill. Perhaps I should have learned that a distraction was a way of quite quickly changing the course of an otherwise difficult argument. More fool me. I still have a lot to learn.

What to Do: Ambiguity and an Open Mind

To remain viable, two contradictory ideas need to have their own separate spaces in your mind. Bring them too close to each other and they will cancel each other out, therefore an 'open mind' is needed. This is how you might accomplish this:

Ambiguity and bubble thinking

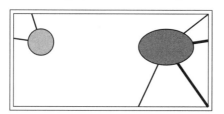

To hold separate bubbles of ideas in one frame of reference requires separate and distinct anchorage points in your mind. Bubble logic needs to be anchored somewhere so that it looks 'reasonable' in some context. We may choose to diminish the importance of any shared reference points. Denial, white lies, distance, alternative explanations or evasion may also be involved in sustaining these two bubbles of reality.

When dealing with or creating quite separate realities, it seems that maintaining a degree of openness toward each of the ambiguous ideas requires a sense of trust in oneself, an intellectual and emotional mobility and in some cases, perhaps selective self-deceit.

Bubble logic becomes viable when supporting reasons for each of the separate realities are strongly held within a separate bubble of reasoning. People who will support and/or collude in maintaining each of the separate realities will be sought out and encouraged. Each reality is then reinforced and firm boundaries erected.

So – You Want to Burst the Bubbles

- You may discover someone or a situation 'out of the character you expected' and 'demand' clarity, for your own sake. However, there may be an equally strong justification in place for maintaining, controlling or submitting to the situation.
- If the alternative ambiguous realities need to be challenged, then the consequences need to be considered first.
- What might appear to be a duplicity or falsehood may in fact be the lesser of two evils.
- Consider the flow of time. A challenge requires the two bubbles to be brought so close together that the reasoning, endorsements and validations break down.
- Supporting anchors in each reality also need to be removed.
- Given that considerable effort is often invested in maintaining separate realities, you should expect considerable resistance, denial and distraction if you attempt to challenge these situations. Some people may be colluding or 'living with' the prevailing illusion and may not want to change matters for their own reasons.

It takes an act of will to maintain two conflicting ideas as 'open'. People may well have a reason, whether honourable or not, for maintaining this level of active partitioning of reality. Two opposing ideas held apart in this manner are expressed as equally valid positions, NOT as either/ or. The individual 'anchors' may give each idea some basis to be true in isolated contexts. Understanding these contexts AND then looking at the bigger context enveloping both may provide an insight.

TIPS

- We can be aware of something; however, it is pragmatic to remember that we are not always called upon to comment, judge or decide. Sometimes the best reaction is to hold your own counsel and not to comment at all.
- Practice withholding a thought or a comment when you feel impelled to make a decision in situations where there is great ambiguity and contradiction.
- Are you making a decision simply to end the tension or do you want the best decision(s)?
- Try to find alternative anchors for the opposing ideas and simply refuse to allow yourself to choose using familiar old reasons for a while.

When thinking about great ambiguities and huge uncertainties, care may be required in testing your own understanding and basic assumptions before any judgement of the truth is attempted.

Uses

An ability to hold apart two contrasting mental states may well have application in many management practices where negotiations are complex, and in managing people with diverse needs. This sort of thinking skill could also be a way of managing ambiguity and complexity.

Overuse

There is a danger in displaying an ability to think and reason across vastly different domains without explanation. We risk our authenticity. Care is therefore needed when displaying bubble logic skills.

If someone else's frame of mind is closed off to your way of thinking and your ideas then it is pointless trying to explain how you see things. An attempt to explain to the other person how he might be able to re-frame inherent contradictions may not always be welcome. You may be mobile in your own thinking but the other person may not be. It is often best to hold your own counsel until asked by someone who is ready to take a wider perspective.

Further Development

For me, this is a very new area that is under development. I would welcome practical advice from people who have been able to transfer this form of mental processing for beneficial positive purposes. Please contact me via the web site: http://www.spreid.com

Module 54

Bubbles, Ambiguity and Lies

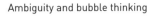

Ambiguity and bubble thinking

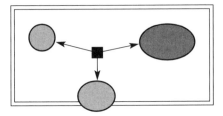

When we are attempting to deal with ambiguous information, some of it will 'feel' right and some will 'feel' wrong.

Some of the information may be badly anchored or beyond the 'boundaries' with which we are familiar. The question then is, 'Are we dealing with an ambiguity or an active attempt to deceive?'

What We See

In the illustration above, a variety of potentially contradictory or competing options may be viewed from a fixed position. Given the perspective of the person looking at these three alternatives, the lower option will intuitively 'feel' wrong. The ambiguous information represented by the lower sphere illustrated above may or may not be a falsehood. Alternatively, the perception of the decision-maker may be simply too narrow to encompass a big enough frame of reference.

What to Do

There are degrees of ambiguity, and then there are lies. A person may genuinely believe in the separate domains as honest and true; on the other hand, she may be unwittingly shielding herself for some reason, or substantial denial may be at work. Ambiguity and convincing lies have some common ground. Both are often incomplete and both have some basis in true facts. 'One trickster's way to disguise a lie is to give the lie an element of truth.'

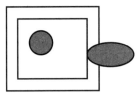 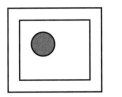

Perhaps the difficulty can be overcome by seeking more explanation and or further exploration. Self-awareness of feelings and intuition will aid the process of mapping approximately where the discomfort sits before an ambiguous option is dismissed out of hand. Sometimes you have to trust your feelings, your instincts. You can always rationalise your decision later when more information appears.

Why This Is Important

We need to avoid being deceived. We still need to learn 'at the edge' and to be able to distinguish truth from falsehoods and mistakes.

TIPS

In dealing with ambiguity, a reasonable self-check is to ask yourself:

- 'Is it me, am I the problem? Is my/our perception big enough to cope with this? Am I being too "square"?'
- Or is this really wrong? (This is a devil of a decision place.) If in any doubt, trust your core values and your intuition.
- Is the distance between ways and ideas too far? Is the other person's thinking literally too far away from your own?
- You might choose simply to agree to differ and walk away.

Use

When faced with edgy information and decisions.

Module 55

New Species Bubble-off: New Directions

Ambiguity and bubble thinking

Sometimes to get full value from a contradictory reality, complete separation is required. The bubble of new thoughts or revolutionary ways of doing things may need to be established to prevent the new clashing violently with the old, or to prevent the two cancelling each other out. A distinctly new frame of reference is formed. To some extent, this happens with parents and adolescents, cats and kittens. Old business sometimes gives birth to new business ventures. They are intentionally set up physically far away from central control.

What We See

The creation of a new frame of reference implies a whole new set of rules, assumptions, experiences and attitudes. In other words, the old frame gives birth to a new one. (A long gestation period and birth pains are images that spring to mind here, followed by an equally turbulent childhood and adolescence, including a turbulent leaving-home period). In business and in home life, sometimes the contradiction between the two apparently viable yet contradictory options may be too disruptive to hold them in close proximity. Cats kick their kittens out. Complete independence arises. In some cases, organisations bud-off new hybrid companies; alternatively, individuals leave to set up their own operations with their own 'rules'. Children leave home. Some emigrate.

From afar we can look at these transitions dispassionately. But for those who are directly involved, passions about the right course of action often run very high. To those rooted in the old world, 'radical' change will feel and be perceived as highly illogical. For the people of the 'old world', it may feel as if their friends have developed a mad idea and set off on an equally insane journey, to an uncertain future. They may even take steps to 'prevent this folly'. Embarking for the thrill of the unknown, other people will invoke a pioneer spirit that they find appealing and invigorating! They don't see threats; they see 'the future'!

What to Do

Step back, take a detached look, smile and send them on their way with your blessing, realising that staying together would be destructive. If you are an organisation, you might consider how this might be accomplished with new ventures.

Why This Is Important

It is the way of evolution. To stand in the way of this powerful force is dangerous and potentially destructive. Sometimes people have to trip up, fall down and get back up unaided in order to learn, progress and move forward under their own efforts.

TIPS

- Consider who or what you may be standing in the way of and review your reasoning.
- Fear tends to hold, freeze, lock, or fix us. When we are locked down we may try to lock others down with us until we feel 'safe'. What do you fear most and are these fears your responsibility alone? Who else is in there with you? If someone else is locking you down what do they fear? What is the truth of the worst thing that can happen in this situation and is the fear-induced energy loss really justified?

Uses

Parenting. Managing and encouraging innovation.

Module 56

Abstract Reasoning

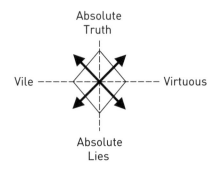

At the beginning of this book we looked at how our minds hold information in a relative way. Cold facts and raw information are held in reference to other data, creating a sense of meaning. Creating new cross-reference points using a logic cross helped create insights.

When we create a logic cross, occasionally there are some stretch points at which reasoning and logic become fuzzy. It would be easy for us to dismiss these too soon. Occasionally some of these will pay off. Some of the relationships and ideas we develop when we clash the unusual can be quite useful. When we are pushing the limits of an idea, it may be helpful to remember that any insights may result in something ambiguous.

What We See

When we cross absolutes that are in practice difficult to realise, we create strange relationships (see the illustration above). When we cross- reference abstract ideas with each other the results may have partial utility. In the example above we see that some or all of the corners of the model will be either impossible or peculiar in some way. This sort of cross I call an 'abstract diamond'. In an abstract diamond the four trend lines that emerge from the centre and head toward the corners can sometimes be named and can create a useful insight.

The model above raises some interesting questions. This particular example would identify that a truly virtuous person may be credibly associated with the top right corner but not normally with the extreme bottom right corner. Similarly, a vile person might seek at some stage to be credible with the truth; however, the top left corner also looks difficult to sustain. On the basis that every good lie contains some truth, a vile person would have to possess some competence with the truth. And in order to remain virtuous, a person must 'know' something of the nature of truth and lies, and of the vile. The diamond on this chart would be irregular and the points at which people are located may overlap in an irregular way, but there would still be some useful insights.

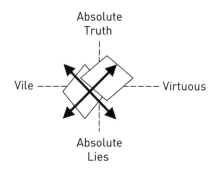

Since none of us are truly vile nor truly virtuous and since few if any of us are given to dealing in the absolute truth or with absolute lies, we could cast a diamond or a square at a variety of points, avoiding the corners, to describe different characters. Notice that in this model the diamonds may overlap. These two characters have some things in common but will clearly be quite different personalities.

What to Do

Cross any two interesting contradictions or absolutes that people hold dear. Remember, the mapping is not confined within a conventional four-square grid reasoning model. The two people represented by the overlapping shapes shown above may share some characteristics. Some of the spaces will seem impossible, while others may illuminate an insight. Repeat the exercise with a variety of crosses until something useful emerges.

TIP

- Dismiss what can be agreed to be absurd, but hold on to anything, no matter how ambiguous, that might provide a useful indication.

Use

For a deeper understanding of complex situations and personalities.

Tuning the Controls

Module 57

Orientation Toward Time

People live and operate with a particular orientation toward time. For example, think of the people who frequently talk about 'the good old days' or those who are convinced they will 'only be happy when...' Then there are people who live here and now and hold no regard for tomorrow.

An unhelpful bias in mind toward the past, the future and the present can be a limitation on performance. It is healthy to review and adjust, and perhaps set a new balance regarding what emphasis and how much energy we allocate to our attitude toward time.

What We See

An idea can hold us in space and time but the world moves ever onward. We may have a future dream and miss the present day. We may have a feeling or a thought locked in the past that feels very real right now, and we miss the present moment and our future for the sake of a phantom. We may be 'here and now' but fail to be concerned for the future and may not recognise lessons from the past. We conduct our lives from different places in time.

What to Do

Gain an appreciation of three orientations toward time. Imagine three people who each seem to spend most of their time with their minds and their behaviour orientated toward:

(a) the past

(b) the future

(c) the present moment, right now

It might be easy to imagine the first two. If it is difficult to imagine how someone might live 'in the present moment', consider small children at play, an artist painting his muse, a hedonist or an enlightened monk. For people at (a), (b) and (c) consider what types of decisions they might take and how they might behave. How would their conversations tend to go?

Now consider where your own bias may be located. Ask how this will affect the way you think, take decisions and act.

- Are you focused too much on the future – for example, work now, live later?
- Are you stuck in the past, remembering the good old days?
- Are you really aware of the here and now?

In reality, each orientation toward time has merits and demerits. No one place is a perfect place from which to think. We do, however, see people debilitated by being locked into just one orientation. The key to living a healthy productive life is to do justice to each of the three attitudes to time AND to possess the flexibility to consciously move between all three.

A Bias for the Past

If your thoughts are strongly influenced by the past, you need to consider whether these influences are useful to you right now. Some 'past orientations' are useful, some not. Our experience – the reason we get the jobs for which we apply and the foundation of our relationships – lives in the past. Some past memories hold us back or are corrosive in some way. It is possible to re-frame, re-classify and adjust a past experience by re-visualising the memories. Past events cannot be changed, but the way we view them can be. We can re-package the past by reconstructing the memory and giving the same events different, positive focal points. Alternatively, if the old memory needs to be parked in neutral for later disposal, re-frame it as now substantially less important.

Are You Waiting for the Future?

'The future' is a classic Western 'middle-class' mindset, in which people invest a lot of their present resources and energy in what 'will' happen next. People suffer privations now for an anticipated payback later. We defer happiness, for example, until we retire, get that job, marry that person, win the lottery, pay off the mortgage or hit some other material target. An ability to think more clearly comes from accepting that you will do your best now and leave what will happen later to faith in your ability. If you do your best here and now, then there is nothing else to be done. Too much concern about the future can seriously blunt attention on the present moment. A fear of losing something or someone can either devalue what you have that is good here and now or can accelerate what has become inevitable.

Punch Through

People often expend vast amounts of concern and energy worrying about future events or possibilities. I have found the idea of 'punch through' very helpful when faced with a seemingly overwhelmingly difficult task that is just over the horizon. The trick when faced with a perceived enormous difficulty in the future is to prepare well and then to aim 'past' the future event. Imagine being in the future, looking back at having already achieved a good outcome. Focus on the desired outcome, not the barriers. This sort of rehearsal helps improve confidence and performance. Athletes have long practised visualising winning before they begin.

Living and Working Here and Now

'In the moment' is a real gift to possess. Watch small children and you will see why. Their play is alive, fully committed and 'in the moment'. They are immediately open to surprise, to their imaginations and to learning. As we age, we seem to drop this level of openness in favour of prediction and pleasure deferred. Sadly, living 'here and now' is becoming a skill that needs to be developed.

'Learn from yesterday, live for today, hope for tomorrow. The important thing is not to stop questioning.'

Albert Einstein

Why This Is Important

A particular time orientation can be a progress-blocker. An ability to place yourself, at will, in any of the three time orientations can be very powerful.

TIPS

- Consider what is good and bad about each of the three orientations toward time. Then consider people you know who live mostly in each of these three spaces. How would a productive conversation proceed in terms of the content, style, rules, roles and behaviours for each of them?
- Know your orientation toward time.
- Do you have an appropriate balance between respect for the past, living in the present moment and preparation for an uncertain future?

Uses

Various; for example: self-development, appraisal of others, negotiation influencing, creating marketing campaigns that resonate with particular points of view. Strategic planning. Life planning. Seeking happiness.

Module 58

Abundance and Shortage Mentality

One of the basic drivers of your thinking is your attitude toward (and beliefs about) the abundant availability or shortage of the things you deeply believe you must have. These beliefs and attitudes motivate your behaviour and therefore the quality of your performance.

You can have deep-seated needs that are obvious and material. For example, you might believe you need money, or a particular house, car or job. However, you should not overlook your deeper fundamental motivations. These might include your need for attention, affection, advice and hugs; for being 'the best', being approved of, being a graduate, a doctor, or a lawyer; for being loved and included; to have power or information, a clear sense of direction or a higher purpose; or any number of abstract drivers of your behaviour. If these deep-seated drivers are seen as 'vital', then your perception of abundance or shortage of availability will cause you to think and behave in ways that may or may not be appropriate or beneficial.

This core programming can steer your thoughts and behaviours long after the need has been fulfilled and surpassed.

What We See

The way you perceive the availability of the things that matter most to you moves you like a compass needle. A few central beliefs are likely to orientate you, your life, your family or your organisation in a particular direction. These central beliefs can skew your thinking, your behaviour and your life.

What to Do

It is smart to figure out what your core needs are. What makes you put in prodigious amounts of energy to secure what you want? Why do you need this now? Then, if what drives you is still worth keeping, make sure you can find ways of perceiving it to be abundantly available. You may need to think more creatively about where you will locate a genuine sense of abundance or how you will modify your drive.

When you believe that what you need most is in short supply you may fight all the harder to acquire or hoard it. The target of your attention then changes into something you hadn't imagined. What may have originally been seen as a genuine need may become greed or obsession. Sometimes the drive creates a sense of purpose or validity. Removing the drive might cause you to question who you are and what on earth you have been doing. For some people, facing such questions can be unpalatable, so they carry on with an old need driving increasingly odd behaviour.

A bad habit within thinking is to follow motivations and behaviours based on outdated past needs. Unlocking this in highly ambitious people may lead to anxiety about 'what to do next' or an admission of wasted time in the past. The former you can overcome, the latter you can dismiss. You will cope. Your basic orientation and your drives can be challenged. You do have a choice to redefine the orientation of your attitudes and beliefs about the availability and scarcity of the things you believe you really need. Start with self-knowledge.

Ten Point Check-out

What is it that you believe you most need that is in short supply?

1 What is 'it'? Describe it clearly.
2 Is it truly unavailable or rare? Or is the item symbolic of something else?
3 Is it still important and if so why? What are the associations?
4 Is it the only choice, and if so, why?
5 What alternatives or other positive options or choices are available?
6 What else is available in big quantities now?
7 We sometimes forget the little things that are always available at low cost or for free. How can you bring these back into focus?
8 What have you overlooked recently?
9 How does new knowledge impact the way you think?
10 How does your personal current orientation help you or hinder you?

Why This Is Important

A particular orientation toward availability can be a progress-blocker or an enabler. An ability to create a realistic 'abundance mentality' can be very powerful. When things are abundant you may feel 'rich' or 'blessed'. It is easier to be generous.

TIPS

- Smart people have a strong sense of themselves, their environment, the other players and of what might become available to them. This is different from what IS available. This is positive thinking, sharp-eyed awareness and optimism at work.

Uses

An 'availability audit' works in many situations, including both your personal and your work life. Consider how you react to changes in budgets, resources, people and markets, as well as the availability of attention, affection or time.

Module 59

Locks, Blocks and Motivators: Inner Messages

Deep within our frames of reference are a good number of 'recordings' or inner messages. Some of these might have made perfect sense at one time but by now may be unhelpful or problematic – past their 'use by' date. For example, someone important in your past may have repeatedly said to you, 'You will never be able to do that…' or, 'You are very clever and you will always be successful in what you do!'

Outdated negative inner messages can get in the way of moving forward. Occasionally we need to rewind, review and replace them with positive, helpful messages.

What We See

A simple example of an old and now unhelpful inner message might be played out when you sit down to dinner as, 'You MUST eat everything put in front of you.' This might have been a good message when you were young and needed lots of food to fuel your growth, but not if your body weight and body chemistry are all wrong as an adult. Unhelpful inner messages at work might include, 'Hard work, long hours equals commitment,' or 'Anyone who leaves early is letting the side down.'

Some people have great messages running in their minds about what fantastic, warm, loving, successful people they already are and will continue to be. Others benefit from a font of unconditional love and forgiveness available to them. Some benefit from knowing they will always have a safety net: a protected place to which they can retreat. Some people feel like they are and always will be in control. Find and hold your own good messages. It is healthy to weed out the ones that don't serve you now.

Know What Motivates You – Identify Your Inner Messages

Many of your important lifestyle and business decisions are driven by your inner scripts and messages, so get to know them. Your inner messages are strongly linked to what drives you. For example, if your deep inner motivations are to be 'rich' or 'not poor', to be 'safe', to be 'a family person', or to 'fully experience life/art/fame', then much of what you think will be processed in relation to these scripts.

As you rationalise a decision, a particular message may be played that underscores why you believe your course of action is justified. You may even find that you use reinforcing statements in conversation. For example, someone who talks about 'killing the opposition', or who frequently talks in terms of 'cut and thrust' might have an inner script that leads him to believe deeply that 'life is all a brutal fight'. Try to figure out what your own inner messages, scripts and drives are. Your everyday language may hold a clue.

Your language, your self-messages and the people with whom you associate reinforce your preferred patterns of thinking. Sometimes the way you 'present' yourself can set up a sequence of thinking, speaking and behaving. The way you think and your attitudes can be shifted in other ways too. Your choice of garments, the vehicle you drive and the environment you choose can all influence the path your thoughts take. Suffice it to say that it is smart to get to know how you process the persistent inner messages by which you allow yourself to be guided. You have a choice.

What to Do

Identify the most common inner messages that seem to shape your life the most. Are these still useful? If not, how will you modify them? Try 'affirmation'. Create a plausible positive statement of what you want in the present tense. Repeat it out loud to yourself, like you mean it, ten times.

Make sure you keep physically fit and that you stay mentally fit by 'swimming in clean positive thoughts' and by choosing to be in the presence of good people and good messages.

Create your own positive inner messages. Avoid people and situations that are persistently negative. You do not have to tell these toxic people what your intentions are, simply be unavailable to them. Be somewhere else.

TIPS

- Ask who is the voice on a recurring inner message. Is it a good message? Is it your own voice or that of someone else? Is the voice friendly? If it's useful, call upon the belief more often, re-affirm it.
- If it's not a friendly, helpful message, try changing the voice. If the voice is hostile change it to something silly such as a cartoon character; it's then easier to ignore! Accord the voice less authority. Dismiss the voice as 'known but unimportant': 'Yes I know you but your opinion no longer counts.'
- Avoid toxic people.
- As the ancient Chinese proverb says, 'If you wish to conquer, first conquer yourself.'
- Get as many psychometric profiles done on yourself as you can. Rarely will one method give you a true dynamic picture of yourself; however, several will give you some good pointers.
- Ask people you respect what measures and inner messages about themselves they have found most useful.

Uses

Improving personal performance. As a starting point for conflict resolution, resolve your own conflicts within yourself first.

Next Steps

Next time you are about to do something important, be self-aware. Try to clearly hear the 'must do' messages without fighting them. Get to know where they spring from if you can. Once they are identified, you can begin to use or dismiss them.

Last Words

It is important to know what holds us back and what drives us forward. Gaining familiarity and control will take time but is worth the effort.

Module 60

Ruts and Rails: Good and Bad Habits

We believe we are a 'thinking species' but much of the time we are employing automated mental patterns or 'mental habits'.

Original thought is hard work and consequently is not so common. When you allow yourself to act out a habit you are running mentally and physically on automatic pilot. You cannot be in a state of self-awareness when you allow your mind to run on an automatic setting. Clearly these habits of mind can impact your performance.

What We See

Some of our thoughts and behaviours become thoroughly embedded. The good thing about some habitual patterns is they make us very efficient at repetitive tasks. Good habits and training help keep us alive when we need to coordinate fast-moving cars, horses or sports activities. A habit of the mind can be a good and a bad thing at the same time.

> *We eventually grind grooves and tracks*
> *along which our minds too readily run.*

Good habits help project to other people that you are reliable and predictable. On occasion, though, you might feel as if you are on rails and cannot get off the same old track. Bad habitual belief patterns don't help you. For example, you might believe you are 'stuck' when in fact you do have a choice. By an accident of birth or education you might find yourself in the 'wrong kind of company' or the 'wrong employment'. You may well have been successful in the past but you might have been happier and more productive elsewhere.

To change yourself and your circumstances for the better may be possible, but it has to involve you taking responsibility for yourself and your actions all along the way, for better and for worse.

What to Do

Know Your Own Ruts and Rails

What you think and believe to be true determines how you behave. If you do wish to change the way you behave you may therefore need to adjust what you believe to be true and the way you think. If you find old habitual routines no longer helpful, you may need to bring them to conscious attention and to make the underlying beliefs explicit so that they can be modified. You can choose to cultivate the good and weed out the bad. There are several ways to make your beliefs and patterns more explicit.

Whilst our physical or behavioural habits might be easy to detect, the ruts and rails that our thinking habits follow are much more difficult to spot. Here are some mental predispositions you might want to review change, or tune:

- Pick a context first, such as 'work', 'health', 'exercise', etc.
- Look out for sentences in which you employ absolute words such as: always, absolutely, never, should, must or will.
- In detecting fixed thinking patterns, look for beliefs that you assume to be 'always' and 'absolutely' true. Adjust your words: always becomes 'sometimes', never becomes 'rarely', and should becomes 'may'. Create mental space for alternative, more flexible beliefs and behaviours.

It can also help to look in your life for recurring experiences. Review them and attempt to find the common elements. Ask why these patterns were engaged or initiated.

- Who was involved?
- Who played what roles?
- What role did you play?
- What (theatrical) props and contexts were set up, ready for the pattern to play out?
- Very important: What were the major assumptions you and others attached to the important parts of your repeating experience?
- And if you were aware at the time that the pattern was now upon you, why did you not act to change its course or stop it altogether?

Another great way to surface your ruts and rails is to listen to people you respect. Try to get explicit feedback by asking for time to discuss how you are. Dismiss nothing until you have had a chance to think through and examine what has been heard. Pay particular attention to ideas and remarks that you find hurtful.

If an emotion has been pricked, pose a series of questions in an open, honest enquiry before you dismiss the comment. Consider in an impartial way:

- What if the person is correct in what she says?
- If she is not correct, then what influenced her decision to say what she said?
- Also, ask yourself, 'What has been my role in leading her to such a conclusion?'
  - 'What might I do to change her opinion of me?'
  - 'Is the effort worthy and worthwhile?'
- Another oblique question to ask yourself is, 'What am I holding on to that I believe is so valuable that what other people say hurts me?'

We all have some scope for change. This will depend on your willingness to change and the amount of effort you are prepared to invest in developing yourself, particularly in regard to the way you make sense of the world, the way you make decisions and the way you act.

Why This Is Important

When we allow locked down, unthinking habits to rule what we do we risk being stereotyped, we may become boring, or worse still, we might be exploited through a predictable weakness. Bad habitual mental patterns may repeatedly draw us toward the wrong type of person, bad working practices and unhelpful situations. We need to constantly weed out bad mental habits and create healthy new ones.

TIPS

- Some of your habits may have taken a lifetime to establish. If you have spotted some personal beliefs and practices that are worth changing it will require time, awareness, support and considerable effort.
- Again, self-awareness is important.

Uses

As part of self-improvement, personal and team change programs.

Module 61

Automatic Triggers

Habitual patterns of behaviour that engage little or no thinking can be 'triggered' without our conscious awareness.

For example, we assume that someone wearing the uniform of authority, such as a cleric, a doctor or a pilot, deserves respect before we get to know them.

When we are 'triggered' we are not self-aware and we are at risk of being exploited.

What We See

Our thinking and behaviour can be shaped by the way we are 'triggered' into responding. Triggers are all around us. For example, we hold respect almost automatically for people wearing the 'uniforms' of a policeman, an army general or an airline captain. We can also be triggered into automatic responses if we resent particular authority figures or if we believe we are the authority figure and we expect everyone else to respect us.

Another trigger is to believe TV, radio, press and web information at face value, as fact, without question.

Groups also adopt 'normal' behaviours. Many members of a group will find their need to fit in with the group overrides their willingness to think or stops them standing up and challenging what the group accepts as 'normal'. Any of these deep inner scripts of what we believe is 'supposed to happen' will trigger our actions and reactions to other people, with little or no thought being engaged.

What to Do

Get to know and question your personal triggers. Ask yourself why you behave 'automatically' as they arise, without conscious thought. Recognise where your own tripwires and triggers are and re-frame the memory from which each one springs. Make that memory less important if you can. Recognise the sequence and disrupt it by thinking and acting differently. If energy is involved, disperse it in a good way.

Affirmation techniques can be useful in resetting an idea in mind to something better. Your mind will take on board something quite quickly if the idea is stated positively, simply, in the present and with belief, especially if you repeat it out loud ten times. The new idea can become a belief if you repeat and consolidate what you say with what you do over time.

Be self-aware as to why you, or wider groups, do things in a particular way. Be especially aware of slow insipid drifts in the wrong direction. Incremental change is difficult to spot or to resist. Listen to people who question what is 'normal'.

Remain alert and self-aware, particularly when in a group in which you sense the ideas or behaviours are wrong. Challenge in your mind what is happening. If it is safe or right to speak, do so. If it is not safe, then discretely remove yourself as far from this group as possible.

Why This Is Important

Living without thought is dangerous morally and physically. Social and economic histories provide examples of how 'group think' is dangerous. Individuals and groups can be deluded into believing that what they are doing is 'right' when in fact they are very wrong.

TIPS

- Comedians are often acutely aware of what many people take for granted.
- Listen to people who live on the fringes. You need not agree with them but they may serve to illuminate your triggers and your mainstream assumptions.

Uses

Self-awareness. Avoiding being duped. Influencing skills. Looking for innovation – finding solutions to problems that people have come to accept without thinking.

Recommended Reading

Influence Science and Practice, by Robert B. Cialdini, is an excellent book. Written more than 70 years ago, *How to Win Friends and Influence People*, by Dale Carnegie, is still really engaging. In addition, take a discerning look at the NLP literature on influence.

Decisions

Module 62

Slippery Decisions: Yin/Yang Lessons

Many problems do not respond to pure logic. When you are faced with 'slippery problems' there may be several interpretations as to what constitutes 'correct' answers. This second type of problem lacks clarity because different interpretations of the same issue are possible.

An example of a slippery problem would be, 'What is the best way to educate our children?' The answer that meets your needs may not necessarily meet mine. With a slippery problem, people may disagree with a solution that meets the needs of others.

Problems of this type are relatively common, particularly in project management, middle and senior management and in our personal relationships. Pure, clear-cut solutions cannot be created for problems of this kind. If we use a simplistic, **absolute** pattern of decision-making to solve this second, more complex class of problem, then our performance, and probably our happiness, are likely to decline.

To help us to more effectively deal with these more slippery problems we will employ a yin/yang image to hold in mind the shape of the problem and the likely outcomes and consequences.

What We See

Recall our decision module from Territory One. When we looked at the pure logic of an absolute type of reasoning, all information regarding the issue fell neatly into a pattern of either right or wrong, or was either on or off. A cleanly divided circle represents this pattern, as illustrated below.

Information is judged

The information
falls into clearly
defined, absolute areas

'Slippery' problems, however, do not fall neatly into an 'either/or' pattern. The distribution of issues looks more like the yin/yang diagram below.

172

Yin and Yang

What to Do

This more complex class of problem can only ever be optimised, since a full, 100% clear-cut resolution is never possible. Answers and solutions will be partial or incomplete. Slippery problems can only be resolved by compromise. With this in mind, several behaviours are required to get a useful result when dealing with slippery problems and their equally slippery decisions.

- The approach to problem-solving must be aligned with the basic structure of the problem itself. Therefore, be aware of the nature of the problem BEFORE working on a response.
- Remember, many of the outcomes of a decision regarding a slippery issue will be partial, political and/or temporary in nature.
- We can be alerted to a slippery problem by the nature of the material: the issues people seem to offer are ambiguous.

To understand how slippery problems can be managed in your mind, employ yin/yang imagery and use the shapes and follow the exercises below:

EXAMPLE

You are asked to develop and implement a new bonus scheme in a large organisation. This means more money and all sorts of people come forward with a vested interest in grabbing some cash from the scheme. All will seek to influence your decision. A bad outcome will harm your credibility.

Use a clean, unmarked yin/yang image as shown at the beginning of this module. Let's say the people who deserve a bonus are in the black area and that those in the white area do not deserve a bonus. To represent your decision, draw a straight line through the diagram. Your goal is to get as much of the black colour on one side of the line as possible. This will create the shape of your decision.

What do you see? What does 'the shape of your decision' represent? Also, what do the smaller circles suggest? Who or what might they represent?

The diagram below shows one option you might have taken with a complex problem.

If your decision was cut in the manner shown above, how would you expect people to feel? On balance, would you have a good or a bad decision? Compare this with the diagram below.

This is a much better-looking decision, since the line representing your decision puts more of the black section on one side.

Lessons

Yin/yang shows us several lessons quite clearly.

If we assume that the dark-coloured domain is what we wish to include, then no matter how we divide it up with our line of decision, some people will always be left out who should be in, whilst other people will be included who clearly ought to be left out! Furthermore, there will be a glaring self-contained issue in the midst of the domain that gets left isolated and unresolved (see the two smaller circles).

Bonus schemes and any sharing of resources decisions often end up looking like this. This is an inherently political environment. A straight cut to the shape of yin/yang does not permit absolute pure and simple solutions. People who do not understand this pattern are unlikely to succeed in any complex or political matters. In ignorance of the peculiar rules that complex matters follow, such people make ill-founded judgements and can carry through remarkably cruel decisions in pursuit of what they believe to be worthy, absolute outcomes.

Another Lesson

The yin/yang model helps provide another insight. In the illustration below I have added arrows to the line that cuts the decision in order to suggest a few degrees of freedom within which optimised results can still be obtained.

In other words, once an optimal response to this kind of problem has been devised, some people or issues will be wrongly excluded. Whichever way the decision is adjusted, the overall result ALWAYS remains a compromise.

Optimize, but decide quickly

Politicians, people in relationships and managers who have to make choices within complex situations can never please everyone all the time. The sliced yin/yang models above illustrate this dilemma quite nicely.

Yet Another Lesson

More study of a subject that fits this particular pattern will not change the overall shape. More data will not change the character of the issue. It will remain slippery. Therefore, the good news is that once you become aware that a problem fits this particular pattern you can make a decision early and quickly. More effort is pointless – whatever your decision it will still be a compromise and the outcome will still be incomplete.

Save Yourself Some More Time

The advantage of being able to spot a slippery problem is that when we know we are faced with one we can save time by agreeing with others about the nature of the issues, and importantly, the likely incomplete nature of the outcomes, before we offer our response. For example, how would you react if someone who was your higher manager demanded a highly detailed, long-term, strategic forecast with a complete detailed analysis of all future risks and opportunities for a volatile market? A knee-jerk agreement on your part would mean you would spend hours, perhaps weeks, trying to comply with a badly thought-out request. In all likelihood, you would not be thanked for what you produce. Wouldn't it be better to either massage your manager's expectations before you begin or to sensitively enter a dialogue over how much sense such a request makes?

Additional Insight

More Complex Still: Yin and Yang Rotate!

(So make your political decisions quickly and move on).

My picture that best gives shape to slippery problems has another twist to it. The picture should not be thought of as static in time.

In other words, to choose an optimum decision and to then fix it down in the rule-book would be wrong because the whole shape can rotate or wobble or rock! The wider context and the players can and do change position AND so do their loyalties. So the decision-making process has to be alert to changes and should be equally flexible in order to constantly optimise for the best outcome. What is currently correct may soon be wrong. For example, in my country there is, at the time of writing, a directive that local communities should burn significantly more of their waste material rather than sending it to landfill sites. There is a whole hornet's nest of difficult decisions and slippery problems wrapped up in this idea. Decisions involving slippery problems are only ever temporary compromises. As conditions change and the system rotates, the same decision can look progressively less appealing.

Yin/yang rotates, as do the seasons. What blesses you in one climate curses you in another.

Why Yin/Yang Is Important

Thinking about the nature of a problem and the likely outcome BEFORE you attempt to work on it can save time and effort. Problems exist in a context, usually with some other baggage attached, and few are simple. Outcomes are determined partly by the mindset and ability of the person(s) working on them and will also depend on whether the problem is clear-cut or slippery.

TIPS

- When thinking about slippery problems, start from the perspective of the supplementary problems that will be created by various solutions. You are going to have to take several decisions at the same time regarding, 'What to do about the main body of people affected by the issue in hand?' and 'What to do about people who have been excluded?' and 'Which solution will minimise disenfranchisement? This is not always easy to tease out, but is necessary if you want to arrive at a productive compromise.

- Outside of a true crisis, when you are faced with a request to act regarding something complex, ask for time to consider the question, even if it is only a few minutes. Always *first think about the nature of the question* and then ask for clarification of the expected result *before* agreeing to comply. Sometimes you might dismiss the question, based on who is asking. However, if you cannot have time to think then a reasonable and assertive challenge at this stage can save wasted effort, especially if the request and the expected result are mismatched.

- Constantly review decisions regarding something ambiguous to see if your conclusions and plans remain viable.

Uses

Many and varied, especially where life is particularly complicated. Problems that have a political aspect. Resolving political problems requires the intellectual agility to balance the needs of different parties with your own needs, to remain viable. Most managers will at some time or other find themselves in a political situation. Family life can get quite political and complex too! Try to see the yin and the yang. Then you may balance your action and reaction accordingly and at the right time and place.

For additional developer or trainer material, please visit **http://www.spreid.com**

Module 63

Polarities

A Polarity Map®

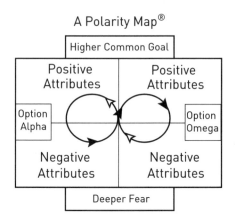

There is a major class of problems that operate in bound pairs. The individual problems cannot be treated separately. Barry Johnson describes these bound pairs as 'polarities'. 'Polarity Management'™ is the term he uses to describe the process by which these are best handled.

For example, organisations often have to struggle with dilemmas and the passions that apparently conflicting alternatives stir in the minds of their managers. The pendulum of opinion as to what constitutes the 'right way' and often 'the only way' swings between such pairs as:

- be big/be small
- centralise/decentralise
- in-house/outsource
- cut spending/invest
- customised/standardised production
- loose/tight

There is a dependency operating between two polar opposites, producing what is described as a 'polarity'. Because of this linkage between two opposing forces or ideas, a number of behaviours can be predicted and a series of typical problem archetypes can emerge.

What We See

Author and all-round good guy Barry Johnson has originated a model that I believe should be taught in every school. Barry is an American author who first published his work on Polarity Managemen™ in 1992 and again in 1996.

The central thesis in Barry's work is that there is a whole family of issues that do not lend themselves to 'either/or' decision-making, where one answer is more correct than the other. Barry says there are problems for which there can never be a clear absolute answer. In the polarity model above, the path people take is always a figure of eight on its side (∞) as one side gains the upper hand over the other.

Barry's concept is very important because his approach in dealing with quite complex problems has the clarity of common sense. We are left wondering why we hadn't seen the sense in his way of thinking long ago.

In reality, each polar point has its own clear advantages and disadvantages. If you find yourself in the negative aspects of one of the poles – for example, negative alpha in the diagram above – then the positive aspects of the other option will present an attraction. Managers often make the case for a transition to 'a far better place' only to discover the disadvantages of the former 'Nirvana'. Suddenly, the old position looks like the right place to be after all! And so the cycle repeats. The same figure of eight pattern recurs, loping diagonally one way, then the other. This is because each issue is seen as a separate problem to be solved when, in fact, both are bound together as one. When decisions have repeatedly been taken to resolve just one side of the polarity as if each side was a separate problem, past decision-making will have the characteristics of a pendulum swinging between two extremes.

A simple example would be the decision to centralise or decentralise control of an organisation or institution. Another polarity is experienced over control and freedom. Another is the needs of the whole group versus the needs of the individual. Elements of both are required to get the best outcomes.

What to Do

Look out for resistant, recurring problems that seem to deny resolution. Situations that persistently resist being clearly resolved might be a polarity. Barry's methods suggest that we cannot resolve this sort of problem with a clear-cut 100%, yes/no 'decision' simply because a polarity is never closed. *A polarity is a loop – a system to be managed – and is not a series of separate problems to be solved.*

TIPS

There are at least three obstacles in our perception that stop people from resolving a polarity.

1 The first is that our minds often find it difficult to capture the whole picture. Given a limited perspective, some people (stuck in Territory One or Two) see only the immediate manifestation and demand an either/or type response. They may even condemn and attack other people who will not take their 'side'.

---

2 Second, we find it difficult, or we do not know how, to leave a decision 'open'; that is to say, generally we like to close off an ambiguity in favour of a defined clear yes/no type decision. This can feed back into a 'make your mind up' mindset of 'choose either this or that'. Clearly, in a polarity this would be wrong and destructive to the whole.

3 A third barrier to our perception is that we fail to see that the two poles require *simultaneous management* because they are intimately connected. Deny one side of the equation and it hurts the other.

Uses

Barry Johnson's model helps us to see a way of getting warring factions from two sides of a conjoined issue to work together. We are now able to manage the two sides of a polarity in a significantly better way once everyone involved realises what they are actually dealing with.

For more information on Barry's models, concepts and methods, I suggest you refer to his book, *Polarity Management*, HRD Press, Inc., 1992, 1996; Amherst, Massachusetts. Or visit his web site, **http://www.polaritymanagement.com**, where you will find a variety of useful tools.

Module 64

Sometimes It Is Best NOT to Choose

Two ideas can be true and equally viable at the same time. It is not always necessary to make a decision, even though we may feel this is required. Sometimes an imperative – driven by feelings – to close down a discomfort caused by an unresolved ambiguity drives us to make a decision too early.

Occasionally it can be advantageous, if a little uncomfortable, to suspend judgement. Doing nothing can sometimes be as good a decision as any other.

'The test of a first-rate intelligence is the ability to hold two opposed ideas in the mind at the same time, and still retain the ability to function.'

F. Scott Fitzgerald

What We See

In many of my workshops I see managers rushing to choose between options. Ambitious managers seem instinctively compelled to argue with people who disagree. By attacking an opposing view they reduce their personal tension between the two ideas and invest greater certainty in one line of thinking in preference to the other. By doing this, they may kill off a viable alternative prematurely AND may miss a chance to develop their ideas beyond a hybrid of the two, or to experience alternative contexts where richer possibilities lie. A decision is a closure. In my experience, haste does not pay dividends in work, in mergers or in our relationships.

Marry in haste and repent at leisure.

Real advances in individual thinking ability occur when people realise that it is acceptable to hold two ideas open at the same time. Both ideas could remain true or useful even if they are opposites, probably in different ways and with different consequences and in different contexts.

What to Do

Rather than assume one idea is right and the other wrong or that one idea is dominant to the other, why not consider both as possibly being correct at the same time? This is the essence of 'slippery logic'.

- Hold the thoughts in mind.
- Suspend judgement – stay 'open'.
- Use terms such as, 'Yes… and…'

Why This Is Important

People often miss an easy trick in dealing with two distinctly different ideas.

TIPS

- Multiple, contrasting solutions can live side by side.
- A choice or a decision is not always necessary.
- Time and energy can be saved by letting go of the competitive instinct.

Uses

During creative or strategic exploration. Living with ambiguities. As a higher order of thinking.

Overuse

Eventually we may be obliged to decide. Too much flipping between alternatives can undermine the confidence of others in us.

Module 65

Context, Problems and Consequences

People sometimes rush into making what might have felt like a right decision but in the wrong context. The consequences then create disproportionately larger problems than those with which they began.

For example, the police may arrest, charge and begin to prosecute the wrong person, with bad consequences all round. Alternatively, the idea may be correct but way ahead of its time. Examples here are Apple's 'Newton', a forerunner of palm computers, or Freddie Laker's 'Sky-Train' that pioneered the concept of 'walk-on/walk-off' cheap transatlantic air travel. Right ideas, wrong contexts.

What We See

Decisions regarding anything of importance are rarely made in isolation and are usually made within some form of context. The context may include a place, a relevant situation, other people and/or a particular environment.

A simple example would be this: You are a manager and are known for your ability to make things happen. People come to you with problems that you usually resolve quite quickly. Your own workload and responsibility increase and your staff continue to come to you with problems. Now step back and consider the bigger persistent problem here. In the first instance, there is a sense of satisfaction in solving a problem; however, a dependency pattern is being set up that is not good for anyone. The solution is to send people away encouraged to devise their own solutions and resolve their own disputes. Whilst this may be slower and may cause some resentment and early learning difficulties for everyone, performance will increase over the long term as individual accountabilities and skills increase.

It is wiser to manage the context rather than the individual issues. Sometimes the context in which a problem sits may be quite complex and there may be of areas of subtle but disproportionate influence. Change even part of the context and the decisions may change completely. Rushing into a decision or acting without reflecting on wider issues may produce unexpected consequences.

What to Do

On occasion, the attempt to resolve one problem leads to the evolution of several more problems of a greater magnitude.

- Therefore, step back and think about the context as well as the problem itself before you consider your move(s).
- Sometimes the best response is no response at all.

- Consider addressing the context rather than the problem itself. Change the context and the problem may change or disappear. The problem(s) that springs up in its place may be more acceptable, more useful.
- Timing is often important.

Set the Agenda

Review the sorts of decisions you and others will have to take over a longer period of time. Make sure you create an environment that gives sufficient time to the different types of decisions that need to be taken. Try to leave a good chunk of time for open creative debate, especially if the decision area involves new contexts or a degree of ambiguity.

Why This Is Important

In fast-moving environments, past experience is quickly invalidated. What once worked may no longer be appropriate. Starting from basic principles or doing nothing until you have re-checked the new context is important.

TIPS

- Make sure people understand the current and likely future settings and contexts.
- Try 'wind-tunnel testing' various decisions if you can before you implement anything. Look for consequences at least several steps along a cause-and-effect sequence.
- Make sure you have not overlooked any new or potentially new participants.

Uses

Decision-making in changing, ambiguous, political or volatile environments. Business and life strategy.

Feeling and Thinking

Introduction

Remember, Territory Three ability is about the extent to which you are able to deal with integrated **pairs** of influences, ideas or concepts.

Head and heart, mind and body are all one.

Like many of the skills proposed in this book, effective use depends upon **a balance** between alternative ideas or tools.

We should also regard emotion and logic as a wedded pair.

Module 66

Physiology and Uplifting Words

'Great! You are fantastic at...'
'I really love you!'
'I believe you can do this.'
'How can we help you?'

'I forgive you.'
'Come and join us.'
'We are doing really well.'

'We will soon be doing even better.'

Words Affect Us More Than We Know

Positive words immediately affect our physiology, minds, attitudes and performance in the same moment. Body and mind are one. Many of us are aware of the positive impact of motivational words but are perhaps less aware of the immediate toxic impact of even slightly negative words on our minds AND our bodies. Negative words immediately influence our physiology. Even low-key words can adjust our physiology. 'Sticks and stones will break my bones, but words will never hurt me,' is a popular children's reply to taunts directed toward them. The saying is actually **not** true. Our physiology changes.

What We See

You can use this knowledge. Improve the body and you improve the mind. Healthy body, healthy mind. Keeping fit is an obvious starting point, but you also need to be aware of the most common words in which you are immersed. Swim in positive words and thoughts and you improve the tone of your mind as well as your body. Performance then improves.

Words can and do hurt. Words and ideas affect your physiology moment-to-moment and this change can actually be demonstrated.

The brain does not differentiate between word pain and stick pain. Pain is pain.

If the pain is abstract in nature, such as the pain inflicted by words, your mind may allocate the pain to a physical part of your body to make you aware you have 'pain'. Psychosomatic or 'referred' pain is quite common. Words clearly influence your physiology. For instance, when someone talks about fingernails slowly scratching on a blackboard or about licking fresh-cut lemons, you get an immediate physiological reaction. Words do immediately alter your physiology, both negatively and positively. So take care of the words you **use** and hear.

What to Do

Create situations in which for as much time as possible you are immersed in positive thoughts and words. Be honest and talk to the positive. Be authentic in what you do. Avoid negative films, activity, journeys or language. Stop using bad or harsh language. Dishonesty impacts you just as much as it hits others. Avoid toxic people and negative situations. Reduce the number of times you read or listen to 'the news' and routine weather checks. Most of what is served up as 'news' is of no real help, and being mostly negative serves no uplifting purpose. Often the urgent way 'the news' is reported raises anxiety levels and releases adrenaline for no real purpose. Avoid being a part of negative practices. Without being materialistic, try to enrich your environment by what you say, uphold and do. Find and fall back on your values when you are in need.

Why This Is Important

We only have one life. Life is not a rehearsal. Life is a very special one-time gift that should **not** be shortened by ingesting toxic food, noxious thoughts or poisonous ideas.

TIPS

- If much of your life is negative, what can you do to change?
- If you have little or no discretion over what can be changed, you can always change the way you think about what is around you.
- Keep as fit as you can, in mind and body, no matter what your age and condition.

Uses

Improving the quality of the way we live and work with each other. Leading and motivating people over the long term. Improving physical and mental health. Wider organisational and social welfare.

Further Reading

Words that Change Minds, by Shelle Rose Charvet. *Working From the Heart*, by Liz Simpson. *The Prophet*, by Khalil Gibran. *Miracle of Mindfulness*, by Thich Nhat Hanh. See also books on 'Tao'.

Module 67

Good and Bad Emotions

Emotions are engaged for a reason. We can learn to use emotions to guide some of our decisions. We need to learn the ability to distinguish helpful from unhelpful feelings and emotional signals.

Emotions have a significant role in the way we think, decide and act. It is therefore important that we have sufficient tools and understanding to channel our emotional energy at home or at work in a productive way.

What We See

Emotions provide hugely valuable information, signalling your well-being, your joys and your fears. Your emotions guide your decisions, even though you may not always admit it. Emotions can have a constructive or destructive influence on your behaviour. An emotion signal – a feeling – may be crude and indistinct: an instinct or an intuition. The trouble is, not everyone understands how emotions work. Perhaps this is why some people do not trust their feelings to guide their decisions.

> *Feelings are always involved when we discover something valuable or when we learn something fundamentally important.*

Your individual ability to deal with and communicate your feelings with others varies too. If the emotion triggered is connected to your instincts to survive, then basic instincts can take you over, quite literally. Your body is immediately armed by adrenaline for 'fight or flight' and rational thinking can be completely overridden by the imperative 'to survive at all cost'. It is smart to trust these powerful instincts when the occasion is right and to wrest rational control back when the body/mind reaction is misguided. You need to be in touch with your emotions and you need to be able to distinguish good from bad.

Emotional Positives and Negatives

If you see emotions as only negative then you are missing part of life's rich tapestry. There are just as many uplifting and inspiring and helpful emotions as there are destructive and belligerent feelings. People have taken snap decisions led by intuition and saved lives. Lives were saved because their deeper survival instincts worked much faster and operated with powerful, urgent action. To dismiss the value of 'emotion' out of hand as irrelevant would be a huge mistake.

Our repertoire of skills needs to include emotional abilities. An expression of emotion between people can be positive and constructive. You build friendships, loyalties and loving relationships with those who are close to you. These emotional bonds buttress you and provide you with strength. There is a whole industry of motivational and inspirational speakers that rely on this human need to share emotional bonds.

Our emotions are relatively crude but powerful forces that have purpose. When faced with a feeling you need to identify what purpose it has – what is it signalling that is important to you? Whilst you are capable of controlling and directing millions of distinct thoughts, you have a much smaller repertoire of emotional signals and much less control over them. You can choose what you do with a thought, but when faced with a compelling emotional signal do you have that much choice?

There are a variety of coping strategies that people may try but some of these are destined to cause problems. I've seen how people try to:

- Enjoy the emotion and magnify the feeling if it is wanted.
- Ignore an emotion if it is unwanted. (When we ignore an emotional signal there is often some sort of rebound later.)
- Defer the feeling (but that leads to 'bottling and mental constipation').
- Resist the feelings and imperatives that come with an emotion. My own experience of resisting powerful emotion is that it can be done but it takes an enormous amount of willpower. The consequence of a battle between head and heart is, like any war, not without cost.
- Divert the energy of a feeling — displacement activity. This depends on whether the alternative is healthy or not.
- Work on changing the associations that trigger the emotional feeling (applies to both positive and negative feelings).
- Go with the emotion, let it have its flow, pick up the pieces later.
- Accept the presence of the emotion but diminish the perceived importance of the feeling — do not be in fear of it. Call your own inner game for what it really is.

You can put down the stick with which you are beating yourself

What to Do

Acknowledge emotional events when they happen, if you are able to. Get to know them, not fear them. Try to develop a sense of how and perhaps where in your body the different emotions begin and what triggers them. This then allows you to head off those that are most destructive by nipping the build-up cascade early on. You can also relax into the feelings that you enjoy sooner if you know yourself.

Get to know what triggers your own adrenaline 'rush'. Review and remove the ones that are clear self-induced adrenaline (drug) abuse. Substitute different routines to help you achieve what you need in life without the urgency. Find legitimate 'excitement' elsewhere. Make emotional expression safe and accepted in the office and home. Take up opportunities to talk about and air your feelings with those you trust the most.

If you are stuck or have difficulty dealing with emotions try this simple exercise. Make a habit of working the phrase 'I feel' into your daily conversation. (Let any steam out in little pops.) Only you know how you really feel, therefore it is up to you to say how you feel so that other people know. If you have a strong feeling it is still OK to say how you feel, right there and then, **BUT** you are not obliged to offer a response there and then as to what comes next.

Why This Is Important

A balance is required in order to lead an authentic human existence involving good communication with and influence over other people.

TIPS

- In business, emotions often can get pushed into the background. Emotional expressions are often preceded by some kind of build-up signals. Being attentive to the other person: halting a logical process early and reverting to addressing emotions rather than logic may help diffuse a difficult situation. If you blunder on in the hope of logically talking your way out, forget it, you will only make matters worse!

- Fear of dealing with an emotion will not make the emotion go away.

- In personal relationships, people sometimes will try to stir up emotions in other individuals they hold strong feelings for, simply to see if the other person still cares or feels in a particular way. Under these circumstances the end point is not about logic. The desired outcome is an emotional engagement, a reaction. The other person wants to witness how you feel.

- There are finite limits to the value of thinking. Sometimes in important relationships, such as with your lover, mostly emotional feeling and less logic is needed!

> *Once lit, an emotional fuse needs immediate and careful attention.*

Uses

Emotional literacy balanced with self-awareness, context awareness, the appropriate use of logic and the right mix of social skills can lead to good communication, influencing and relational experiences. Balancing your life experience. Motivating and leading people in a productive way.

Overuse

Not everything requires an emotional contribution. Some parts of the world are quite sterile and devoid of the need for the emotions. There may be risks of being seen as overly dramatic and not being taken seriously.

Under-use

The Risk of being seen as a cold, insensitive, anti-social clod; with consequent risk of being left at the margin of society.

Further Reading

If Life is a Game, These are the Rules, by Cherie Carter Scott, Hodder and Stoughton. *Don't Sweat the Small Stuff – and it's all small stuff*, by Dr. Richard Carlson. Also see Rick Semlars' book, *Maverick*. He tried a smarter way.

Last Words

What constitutes too much or too little emotional involvement is not for me to define. I'd be a fool if I tried. Suffice it to say that we should try to be socially and emotionally literate, as well as sensitive to the situation and the needs of others. *Give help to people when you can.*

Relationships

Module 68

Self-awareness and Active Separation

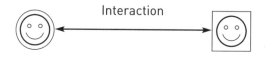

Interaction

When we interact with someone else, we do so without thinking about how many assumptions or what processes are in play within the encounter. An interaction with another human being is never simple. When we interact we do so on many levels; there are at least three possible levels of interaction. We should be mindful of what particular process is being employed during any contact. This model integrates the logical and the emotional, self-awareness AND context awareness in one process. I call this '**active separation**'.

What We See

Interactions can be split into three layers

Relationship
Emotions
Transaction

When we are thinking fast on our feet – for example, during a negotiation or a conflict – we can get a good result if we remember that several separate forces are in play at the same time and that we must stay in sync with what is important. Failing to recognise these forces or misunderstanding the sequence in which they tend to play out will seriously reduce the chances of getting a good result, either at home or at work.

Active separation reminds us to disentangle the component parts of our interactions with others. We can also watch ourselves engage our thoughts at each level.

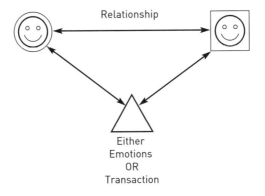

Either
Emotions
OR
Transaction

What to Do

Develop the skill of active separation. Make a serious effort to be fully aware of your own thinking, as you are thinking. Separating awareness of emotions from engagement of emotion in a transaction is part of the process. But this does not mean you become cold and devoid of emotion. By being able to stand back, to overview without being swept away by events, yet being still actively involved, allows you to take in a large amount of information and to act judiciously. This level of involved detachment can help you spot the rules of the games in play and the process patterns.

Why This Is Important

We can fail to communicate due to mismatched expectations and a misunderstanding about what is actually being transacted. Possession of the ability to distil out the layers of complex communication as it happens is a powerful basis for making intelligent decisions. This active self-awareness enables you to decide on your choices, which in turn can help you lead a smarter life.

TIP

- Awareness of something is not the same as an ability to deal with it. Awareness is a positive first step that allows you to know what is happening, where your own limitations are and where you need to build competence.

Uses

Better communication. To generate better interactions between people. To help us deal with challenging conversations by making the layers of communication explicit.

Overuse

On occasion we need to be aware 'but not engaged'. We just need to 'be'. The first statement is a clear contradiction and to some this might sound silly. The second statement aims to clarify the contradiction.

Next Steps

The next time you have a chance to witness an interaction between people, try to observe what is being communicated and whether or not the various layers of signals are being picked up. Then, in one of your conversations, try to read which layer is in operation – in your mind **as well as** in the conversation *as each takes place.*

Last Words

This is a skill worth developing. To be effective, it requires several social skills as well as intellectual dexterity.

Further Reading

See the module on conflict. Find and read books on 'Transactional Analysis' (TA).

In terms of general awareness, there is a whole raft of books on 'NLP' (Neuro-Linguistic Programming) into which you might delve. Some of the literature under this heading can be idiosyncratic, but if you are selective there are some really good nuggets to be had.

For higher levels of awareness regarding other people and their body language, see Allan Pease's most recent books on body language.

Module 69

Staying Clear-headed During Conflict

Our ability to think clearly during the course of a verbal conflict or a heated discussion may be compromised in a variety of ways. Productive, creative conflict requires just as much discipline as good logic and emotional sensitivity. These thinking and behavioural skills can be learned. You can learn to think on your feet during a heated exchange.

What We See

Have you ever left a conflict and come up with the right thing to say some time afterward, when the opportunity to say what needed to be said had passed? Our ability to think clearly may be inhibited by many things. We may, for example:

- lack experience or relevant information
- feel threatened
- feel emotionally sympathetic to someone who needs a firm hand
- feel guilty about giving someone a (needed) hard time
- have unrealistic guidelines about who is allowed to say what when

When we are faced with conflict or challenge, a variety of rational and non-rational influences can come into play at the same time. This turmoil can confuse and limit our ability to think. We can unscramble and map these influences and learn to deal with each in turn. In order to do this we require a relatively strong introspective mental skill to operate *at the same time as* our active involvement in a critical situation. I call this '**active separation**'. (See previous module).

What to Do

There is no strict formula for handling conflicts and emotional events; but in general terms, you should stay self-aware and remain aware of the other person's level of operation.

Thinking, feelings, expectations, motivations and behaviour are all intertwined. If we fail to acknowledge this, then any appreciation of how we think will be stunted and dull. There is a basic human need to engage emotions in a meaningful way.

> ### *Spot the Type of Emotional Game in Play*
>
> *There are many honest emotional events that need to be expressed, but there are some situations where no amount of effort will move the transaction process back into the realm of rational thought.*
>
> - *Some individuals enjoy the emotional realm and feel they have an advantage there.*
> - *Other people feel more in control when swimming in their favourite emotional soup, whilst others simply do not want closure and enjoy the raised levels of attention emotional outbursts provoke.*
>
> *Under these circumstances, it might be best simply to let go of the connections. Your commitment to a relationship should not be entirely unconditional, otherwise you may be held hostage to it.*

Redirect the Force of Conflict

People enter conflict because they feel passionate about something. If you can realign that passion it can become a powerful force that works for you instead of against you. Once redirected, a source of conflict can become a synergistic and powerful energy source.

Why This Is Important

In any demanding environment, including the home, conflict is inevitable. Poorly managed or denied conflicts serve no good. Getting past a conflict in a constructive way can set new, more productive ground rules and can improve relationships.

TIPS

- Never tussle with a pig, you WILL get dirty and the pig enjoys the dirt.
- A conflict should always be about the issue or the feelings, but never about the fundamental relationship. You may have an issue about a behaviour within a relationship, but the relationship itself is never in jeopardy.
- If during the course of a negotiation or a conflict, a friend or a business colleague states that the future of your relationship is on the line unless he gets what he wants, then you need to stop the process and examine this tactic closely. If he does not change his stance, then you need to consider whether the relationship is on the right footing.

Uses

Most competitive environments involve conflict over resources, time, attention and inclusion. This applies in the home and in high-powered negotiations.

Overuse

If every transaction is turned into a conflict, people will avoid you, not include you. Life requires a balance of several different negotiation, concession and conflict strategies.

Next Steps

Find out what your conflict preferences are. Observe and learn from the ways different people deal with conflict.

Last Words

Conflict will not go away simply because you don't like it. Get some training; get used to managing conflict as a skill. Have a bridge-building skill or repair strategy as a necessary complement.

Further practitioner and management team consulting material is available via the web site, **http://www.spreid.com/book**

Further Reading

Getting To Yes, by Roger Fisher and William Ury. *Getting Past No*, by William Ury. *The Third Side*, by William Ury. *Resolving Conflict*, by Shay and Margaret McConnon.

Winning Philosophies

Module 70

Bound Pairs

A central skill of a high-level ability thinker is that which involves keeping two ideas in mind at the same time and remaining functional. An awareness of what 'bound pairs' are and how they operate is equally important. It is a good idea for you to consider how you will cope with these opposing forces, dilemmas and contradictions. Developing your own personal performance philosophy regarding inseparable pairs might help you remain sane when the situation looks crazy.

In order to get the performance you want in the face of complex, demanding bound pairs of problems, knowing what you **will** do is just as important as knowing what **you will NOT do**.

Reflecting on a variety of pairs might be informative. You may find that when you look closely, each situation may carry both a strength and a weakness at the same time. Increasing one increases the other. Paradoxically, 'fixing' a weakness may actually debilitate or fundamentally change a strength.

For example, a person who believes she is assertive and who requires this skill to accomplish difficult tasks in demanding environments may be seen as unnecessarily aggressive in other situations. The more affirmed her strength is, the larger the weakness may become. A similar pattern may emerge in commerce.

When you can appreciate the linkage between bound pairs of characteristics in yourself, then it becomes easier to grasp the same idea in operation in the wider world. When you can detect and accommodate this duality, this pairing of forces into one inseparable coupling, you will have begun to consolidate your Territory Three mental ability.

What We See

In order to cope with our bound strengths and weaknesses, we at least need to be self-aware enough to know what these are and what the associated consequences of inappropriate use are. Dealing with different challenges may require you to switch the way you think, using different models, attitudes and behaviours at different times. Whilst you may be comfortable in making some of these transitions in styles, it is worth remembering that other people may not be. That will impact how they see you and how they behave in regard to you.

Switching between quite different mind sets can be difficult: for example, from 'challenging' to 'calm'. Some people have mental and physical **'wash out'** periods to allow themselves to make a transition to a different state of mind. Some people create and maintain displacement activities to get rid of a particular mindset before they enter a meeting, for example, or before they return home from an aggressive work climate to their loved ones. Some people play intense sport to diffuse their energy or to build it up after a dull office day. I have seen a male director colleague 'pump up' his aggression levels by repeatedly clenching his fists before an intense meeting. Whatever approach you choose, in order to live an effective life a balance needs to be maintained.

Other examples of bound pairs include the yin/yang model. Also, Aristotle's idea of virtue ties in with the concept of bound pairs. Remember the idea of 'connection' between things to guide your thinking.

What to Do

Spend time spotting common dualities, bound pairs, dilemmas and clear contradictions. Consider the pattern they follow – how do these translate or 'cross over' to different situations? For example, issues sometimes present as if they are entirely a huge problem or a major opportunity; however, if you step back and consider each situation, you may see that each has an element of the opposite characteristic.

- Be aware of the other side of your strengths. Hold a balance – a 'Golden Mean', as Aristotle suggests. Weaknesses may be re-framed to become advantages; problems can be turned around to become opportunities.

- Have a range of behavioural abilities and perspectives upon which you can call. (If your only tool is a hammer then most problems may appear as nails.)

- The power of your opponents can be turned by getting them to use their 'strength' in the wrong context. Be aware that they in turn may do the same to you. Damage by one's own hand is most injurious.

TIPS

- Be self-aware, especially when other people attempt to 'fix' a weakness they say you have. If it is a weakness in isolation, go ahead and better yourself, but remember – if this is a bound pair then a strength may be undermined.

- Do not put aside the advice in the module, but take this habit to mind and practise it.

Uses

As a self-awareness technique. In building self-esteem. In seeing different aspects of complex situations. In overcoming adversity.

Overuse

Not all situations are complex nor two-sided. For example, it might be a waste of charity to assume there are any redeemable strengths in the weaknesses of an 'uncouth yob'. Sometimes a yob is just a yob. Sometimes a bad job or relationship doesn't get any better by solving the complexities – it remains just a bad job or relationship. Consider a simpler solution.

Dilemmas are coupled problems that need careful management. I can also recommend that you take a look at the work of Charles Hampton Turner and Fons Trompenaar in regard to their books on how different people and how generally different nationalities deal with dilemmas. Their research is informative and based on several thousand people.

Module 71

Humour and Ambiguity

Sometimes if we don't laugh we may be forced to cry. Huge amounts of tension can be generated by contradictions, dilemmas and ambiguous situations. We may perceive 'tension' as a form of pain, and since we are deeply programmed to avoid pain, this could reduce our mental effectiveness in dealing with complex situations. If we can adapt our perception to one of pleasure, then a particular ambiguity can become easier to live with, and possibly pleasant.

People who are consistently good at dealing with high levels of tension often have healthy coping mechanisms. Timely humour is a powerful energising mechanism for defusing tension and raising spirits. It is therefore a legitimate life and work skill worth acquiring. Laughter has a tremendous healing power – it's a great antidote to grim focus and stress!

What We See

When tension is present, we are operating at the edges of our frames of reference. Emotions are always connected to the edges of our frames because we are stretching the points at which we feel safe and secure. Anger, anxiety and humour are all possible. Skilled people can read the level of tension and cause people to laugh before they cry.

If we know the tension will not go away then we have some choice over how we might react to it; we can modify our reactions.

> *Managing ambiguity can be viewed as a battle to balance opposing forces. One can either suffer the tension that ambiguity creates or learn to enjoy it.*

This particular edge is quite an unreasonable place to be. Most senior directors, many researchers, leading edge artists and lovers will recognise this uncertain place. At the edge, we face elation or despair. This is reflected in the way some people try to manage their way through periods of ambiguity. Some try a playful approach, where others inflict a serious and increasingly aggressive style as a way of dealing with uncertainty. I believe a timely 'sense of humour' is a must on any CV.

What to Do

1 Be aware. What things strike you as ridiculous – yourself included – when you are in ambiguous territory? Can you magnify these to make them even funnier?

2 Be aware that people's tension levels will be higher than normal. A well-placed witty remark can defuse the tension. Suggest how someone from a well-controlled environment might react if they were with you now. (Can you imagine the Pope, the Imam, the King or Queen, our CEO, your grandparents or the Prime Minister doing this?)

3 Understand that any new rules you find may soon be out of date and are likely to be replaced by a new set of incomplete rules. In an ambiguous space, it is possible to make the rules up and see if they work. You can invent humorous stories based around the most ridiculous new rules and behaviours you can imagine.

4 Buy and collect funny books and articles. Some of the material may help you develop your sense of humour.

5 Try attending one of the worldwide laughter clubs set up or inspired by the Indian guru of laughter, Dr. Madan Kataria. You will find it possible to laugh at literally nothing – laughter just for the sake of laughter is really beneficial.

6 You need to be mentally and physically fit to operate in an ambiguous environment, because there is no respite in 'the routine', because the routine does not exist – all boundaries are temporary, incomplete and subject to change. Solid, reliable boundaries are just not available in ambiguous territories.

Why This Is Important

An ability to use humour can help you demonstrate good social and leadership skills, as well as the ability to deal well with ambiguity. Humour is a vital part of an amorous relationship.

Uses

If you have the energy, a sense of fun and a bag of tools that will allow you to function, to stay and to take useful decisions where others simply flounder, you will be better equipped to make major life or strategic business decisions than most people. For staying sane in a demanding world. With the right level of sensitivity and timing, humour is great at defusing anger and tension. For keeping spirits up, despite adversity. In seduction and influence. Used politically, humour can undermine or build reputations.

Overuse

Too much humour, bad timing or poor delivery and you'll look foolish, perhaps insensitive.

Further Reading

Orbiting the Giant Hairball – A Corporate Fool's Guide to Surviving with Grace, by Gordon MacKenzie. This is one of my favourite books. Look also for books on 'invective' (witty rebukes) – these are entertaining in their own right, but may also provide you with some raw material. In such books you may find Winston Churchill's and Lady Astor's exchanges very amusing.

Last Words

There is another balance issue here. Teams and organisations want the best level of performance, but discipline, control and rigour tend to drive out the fun and with it a great source of energy. Of course there is a need for serious control and accountability, but successful organisations need 'hearts AND minds'. To add in legitimate **fun** introduces a level of ambiguity that perhaps a few 'narrow over-focused' people cannot cope with. I would estimate that profitability goes up briefly when the narrow minds have control and down soon after, as the appetite for life drains away. Equally, if hedonists and clowns have control, performance may take a dive too. A higher level of ***managed ambiguity*** is the price of higher performance.

In the past, 3M managed to get this balance about right. 3M induced a counterbalance to the fun-killers by repeating stories of people who beat the serious system and made the company successful – despite the controls. One of the best insights into prevailing philosophy at 3M in the mid-nineties comes from top R&D executive Dr. William Coyne in a pamphlet, *The UK Innovation Lecture 5/3/96 – Building a Tradition of Innovation* (British Department of Trade and Industry). 3M has in the past sustained a long history of solid innovation and perpetuated their own success story. No doubt, new stories are being created there right now. It will be up to a few clever executives to make sure the climate fosters the right ones.

Territory Four

Mountain Tops and Clouds

Arrival

Territory Four ability might be argued to be Territory Zero. To repeat a few lines of an earlier module, we are born with a blank slate and in a state of pure innocence and we do not judge. In a sense, arriving at the higher levels of performance we come to realise that we have rediscovered our earlier state of open innocence, ready to deal – in the moment – with what life presents to us. At a higher level of consciousness, few things require judgement and few things or people are able to judge or master us. It is a simple place where we can be aware of paradoxes but untroubled by the contradictions they contain. However, a higher level of consciousness does not mean we have an excuse to exclude ourselves from the obligation of taking necessary action. The best way of thinking about reaching the rarefied atmosphere comes from a Vietnamese monk, Thich Nhat Hanh:

> *Before enlightenment, I washed dishes.*
> *After enlightenment, I washed dishes.*

Nothing changes in reality. We still must live our lives, but we may live, think and perform from an enlightened perspective.

If you have mastered Territory Three, then by now you will be relatively comfortable with quite high levels of uncertainty and ambiguity, which many people cannot tolerate. Enhancement of ability at this higher level is largely about YOUR philosophy and perhaps a few tools that might come in handy for thinking through disconnected ideas or really complex dynamic situations.

'Return' Journeys and Slippage

Like all muscle-developing activity, regular exercise is required to maintain 'tone'. We can slip from great heights. It can be exhilarating, having reached a dizzy height, to then look around. For some people such heights can turn out to be cold and lonely. If that is the case, the trek downhill will most likely involve some of the experiences gained on the way up. However, we cannot return to our origins and be the same as when we left. The journey changes us.

A desire to make a 'return' may be founded upon an illusion. Any 'return' path must be made with care and with awareness.

Upgrade Your Models and Tools

Module 72

The Onion Map

A tool for dealing with unstructured information

The big onion
(A context map)

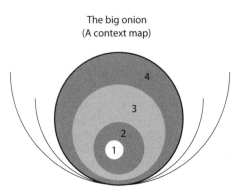

People and things tend to exist in relation to each other. This particular model shows a series of relationships within concentric circles that radiate outward from a starting point. Think of this as a Russian doll: one idea, relationship or thing fits inside another. For example, I exist in a village, within a district, within a region/country/continent/world and so on. This tool serves to help us detect blind spots in our thinking about foggy problems that seem to have no clear beginning or end.

What We See

We think most efficiently when we have information held in relation to other information and when we have some sort of clear boundaries. The ideas behind this particular tool are not new. The Onion Map uses the same artistic representations employed by Dante and Botticelli in their depictions of 'Inferno'. These shapes were used more than 500 years ago to make sense of something as difficult to grasp as heaven and hell. The artist Botticelli, in the period 1480–95, created a series of images showing interrelated territories based upon Dante's 'Divine Comedy'. Botticelli's images suggested that in an ascent to heaven, progress is made through higher and higher interrelated circles. Also, Dante's epic poem 'Inferno' employs the same structure again, with one circle held within another, only in this case each circle describes a step deeper into hell.

Whilst Dante took on the ideas of 'heaven' and 'hell', many of us have difficulty thinking through issues closer to home, such as the reality of a business issue, a personal crisis or something to do with relationships and change. The problem with reality is that it can be too big to grasp. The Onion Map can be helpful in this respect in several ways. It is particularly useful in the early stages of dealing with ambiguous or uncertain situations. The map looks at how things relate to each other and can help us define the territory and any potential blind spots. See the case study below concerning light bulbs.

What to Do

When we are dealing with ambiguous starting points, this model can help us to save time in dealing with unstructured questions and to define the true scope of an enquiry. When we employ an Onion Map, we apply structure to the question first and then slot possible answers into its format. Consider an open question such as, 'List as many reasons as you can why a person left Munich and never returned'. It is an open question, therefore the answers, if any or many, are also likely to be open-ended. We begin by labelling our circles from the centre outwards as:

1 the person
2 friends, family, work colleagues
3 the area
4 the country, etc.

Then populate each with reasons.

An Onion Map may be used to chart out a business and its connections. An onion has many layers.

For further practitioner details and guidelines on using this particular tool, visit http://www.spreid.com/book

Why This Is Important

This model can explain how things fit together and how sometimes our personal boundaries may be illusory or set too close to be useful. An Onion Map is a fast way of dealing with unstructured information. Onion Maps can speed up thinking about layered, complex relationships between things and people. Without one, people may rely on a haphazard approach to dealing with complex issues and they may miss something important.

Uses

As a quick way of mapping close relationship patterns. This tool does **not** provide 'right' answers, but it is quite good at helping to detect areas of work or of our lives that may hold blind spots. For strategic planning.

CASE STUDY

A household manufacturer produces light bulbs for 50 cents and he sells them for a dollar. Initially successful in zone 1 of his context map, our manufacturer expands to sell into zone 2. In order to fully utilise his factory, he enters zone 3, which represents the rest of his country.

Context map and boundaries

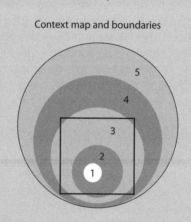

Our light-bulb maker knows his home market backwards, inside out and upside down. As the current leading supplier, he decides not to supply the whole country because the logistics and investment decisions simply do not add up. In other words, he has established an edge, a boundary around a market that he believes he dominates. His current distribution reaches insignificantly into zone 4, but these recently have been problematic customers, few in number who seem to be more trouble than they are worth. They complain they cannot sell his product. Our manufacturer is quite happy though, because 99% of his current customers are very satisfied.

Because our household light-bulb maker is focusing hard within his own terri-tory, he has missed a dynamic new competitor in an adjoining country who is moving rapidly from zone 5 toward zone 4 and the centre with a product that is more efficient and much cheaper to produce. By failing to watch the big pic-ture, our original household light-bulb maker stands to get wiped out by a new competitor. The original manufacturer's downfall will be his assumption that he knows all he needs to know about 'his' market. He has set his boundaries too close to home. The faint voices from the few small dissenting customers at the edge of his business, in zone 4, were warnings to be heeded despite initially high customer satisfaction.

Tuning the Controls

Module 73

Thinking and Doing Energy

More on self-awareness

We possess a finite amount of physical and mental energy, yet our ambitions and our misplaced sense of obligation and loyalty often know no boundaries. In consequence, people can win their battles for the best-paid jobs but lose the very essence of living a real life.

What We See

Western society is getting more frenetic and overloaded. Unhealthy stress levels are increasing. We see poor lifestyle choices affecting physical health; for example, obesity, once rare, is now quite common. Our minds are taking a similar battering too. Mental exhaustion and burn-out from overwork is increasing and tired older parents consider it acceptable to seek calming medications for the children they cannot cope with.

When I set up my business, I drew the logo above. It shows people pushing at a wall. If they stopped pushing and looked around, they would see other people and other easier ways of getting done whatever job they think needs doing. My observation today is that the simple act of 'stop, look around and think' is not happening, perhaps because people seem to have an idea that being 'faster' is synonymous with being more effective. People seem to assume they must work harder – alone – to do their best. Often they will exclaim, 'But I don't have time to stop and find a better way!'

What to Do

Stop the shop – look around. Question what you all do. Figure out an easier way for all of you. This is what I do when looking for performance improvement. Effectiveness is a matter of balancing your energy output to produce the maximum impact. Anyone who attempts to do everything and control **ALL** things is foolish. Therefore, a good question to ask yourself at home and at work, 'What will I *NOT* do?'

Time management and the creation of space in which you have some discretion and control are essential. If you are overworked, a day or two off will not fix your fatigue or a bad system. Work to change and adapt the system in which you operate so that it is healthier and more productive. If you cannot, leave and work somewhere better.

Mental fitness requires a healthy variety of inputs AND sufficient real resting – not just 'snack-break rests' or 'power-weekend breaks'. Take long, meaningful rest periods after times of intense activity. For example, if you can, once every five years try to get a long (three-month) sabbatical or some kind of 'mental time-out'. If you get laid off, turn it into a fantastic opportunity to fulfil important, but not so urgent personal needs and desires.

Why This Is Important

You simply cannot perform at high levels if you are exhausted. Life needs to be a balance between work and play.

TIPS

- What do you enjoy most in life? When did you last indulge this and did you actually enjoy it? When was the last time you explored a new pleasure?
- Have you corrupted a leisure activity; for example, by turning it into a chore or a money-spinner?
- The best way to overcome fear of layoff or an enforced gap in employment is to plan and prepare for it. Save up a cushion of money and resources to tide you through that which may be inevitable.
- Harness your mental and physical resources as you would any other valuable resource. Spend these wisely.
- Draw a life curve. Divide it into four segments. Be honest as to how the curve will flow and where you actually are. Then manage your time and energy accordingly.

Use

Clear thinking and mental fitness.

Next Steps

Check your work/life balance with the people that matter. Insist on taking your leisure time – for everyone's sake. Take a look at the more recent generation of time-management ideas on adopting a wider perspective on managing a lifetime, including important personal and family goals alongside work goals.

Last Words

If you work a 50-hour week against a 40-hour contract in one year, you will make a non-refundable, never-to-be-returned donation of 500 hours of your leisure time! That is equal to 62 working days given for free. Does this earn extra pension or promotion points or does it budge you closer to the edge? Is the system in which you work inefficient or is it exploiting you? Perhaps long hours have become an unthinking ritual. What does this say about the leadership? If you are leading, what does a pattern of individual and team overwork say about you? How much 'extra' effort is too much?

Decisions

Module 74

Place Your Bet and Move On

You may be expected to take a variety of decisions within a range of uncertainties. At Territory Three you will have become used to the idea of living with ambiguity and accepting that many situations involve incomplete outcomes and compromise. Having risen through Territory Three ability, you will already know that making complex decisions requires a blend of your thoughts AND feelings aided by your choice of models, filters and templates. A higher level of decision-making than this involves a higher level of philosophy. A personal philosophy helps when you are called upon to think in this particular realm of difficulty.

Decisions at high levels of uncertainty are a gamble – a bet – and because of this, you will not 'win' all the time. When you do 'win' at this level, your victories will probably be incomplete and complex. Take heart, therefore, when things go 'wrong': you are not alone in making such mistakes. Anyone who has risen to this level of intellectual agility and skill should be able to tell you more than one personal disaster story.

There is no right way or wrong way to arrive at decisions when the situation is highly ambiguous or uncertain. There are no best models to use either. Many of the decisions are already taken.

Even when you possess the skills
to use even the most complex models
and when all your advisors have said their piece
it is up to you.
Place your bet
and
move on.

Module 75

Multarities™

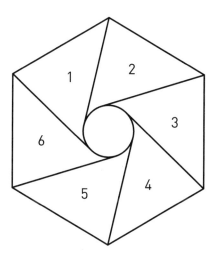

Barry Johnson went on to expand his ideas on 'polarities'. You may recall that a polarity is comprised of two quite different, often opposing forces that are interconnected AND dependent upon each other. Working with a colleague, Barry coined the term 'Multarities™' to describe complex situations as a series of **interconnected interdependent polarities**. Working with a multarity involves working with linked pairs of polarities. When dealing with a multarity, the rules found in a polarity apply to the interconnections. In the illustration above, six polarities are interlinked.

A multarity is a leading-edge concept that allows us to deal in a more competent way with complex situations.

What We See

The most complicated thing human beings have to do in their lives is to relate to other people. Leading a large number of people therefore requires exceptional thinking and decision-making ability.

Many situations require a leader to have the ability to step back and take a holistic view of **all** the forces at work AND the relationships between these forces. When a leader wants to drive through significant change, there will be many different dilemmas, polarities and competing propositions. There will most likely also be a multarity, i.e., *a series of **interdependent** polarities*. Gains made in one area cost in another area. A leader's job is to strike a series of balances for the overall gain to work.

The model helps to make sense out of quite complex situations. A multarity map allows people to see how to balance and reconcile seemingly separate competing priorities into one cohesive way forward. A multarity model allows a leader to align his people with what needs to be done.

What to Do

Understand how polarities work first. Polarities are a simple form of interdependency. (See module 63.) Within Multarities™, a single polarity is always one part of a pair. Just looking at one particular polarity within a multarity is an incomplete look – just as looking at one pole of a polarity is an incomplete look. When faced with a multarity, removing any one of the interdependent parts would lead to the others not being sustainable over time.

Involve others. A multarity model captures and reconciles multiple levels of complexity. For this reason, a number of people need to get involved simultaneously in using this particular model. Since complex situations tend to be dynamic, stopping the shop, freezing processes, gaining an understanding of the interconnecting forces, exploring new options and then agreeing best ways of creating new rules and conduct will be required to get a result. Ultimately this is a large-scale change intervention tool.

Why This Is Important

The multarity model provides an integrated map of the complex balances we need to strike when we are dealing with change.

TIP

- Handling a multarity well involves the active engagement of multiple stakeholders working in harmony to align complex interests and forces. Coercive or directive leadership alone is probably not going to realign a multarity. If you would like a list of practitioners in this field, please contact me via the web site **http://www.spreid.com**

Use

Making a complex change program happen.

Further Reading

See Barry Johnson's web site, **http://www.polaritymanagement.com**

Feeling and Thinking

Module 76

Being

Who are you? Why do you do what you do? Are you really committed to what you are doing?

If you are unsure, then your personal energy is left in conflict and does not flow freely. If you have not understood yourself and resolved your conflicts then you will place obstacles in your own path.

There are moments in your life when everything flows freely. You are authentic and aligned. It is a fantastically calm, assured place.

'Being in the moment' is actually two statements in one, namely, a state of being + presence = in the moment. It does not imply inaction.

The result of what you are doing is already positive before you begin. The ten-pin strike, the hole-in-one, the goal, the target are already won before you move. All are then achieved with ease and flow. This state of being is not a trick either; you really feel you are connected to the flow of things.

Having mastered the process of thinking, the higher levels of performance involve a deeper inner journey that ends up in simplicity: being. There is no question of 'arrival' or closure though, because your sense of awareness is switched to 'always on'. Your state of being is then just part of everyday life and all that it brings and all that you find; you continue being and doing. All that has changed is the manner in which you live, think, say and do things.

Recommended Reading

Look for books or essays by Eric Fromm on having vs being. There are many books available suggesting how and why you need to 'be' a particular way, but my view is that you should make an active choice for yourself. One of many different books I have enjoyed is Jack Kornfield's *A Path with Heart*. Ask what other people recommend.

Module 77

Ritual and Reason

There is a potential danger in being seduced by ritual into accepting without question what is being transacted and the papering over of flaws in reason. You may find yourself indulging someone else's ritual of the annual business strategy review in which the procedures serve to bury heads deeper in the sand, or perhaps the ritual family holiday or the ritual of daily living. Alternatively, you might one day find yourself involved in a ritual of a cult or sect or group of people with particular beliefs. Whatever the ritual, you should always remember the importance of self-awareness. If you are taking part in any kind of ritual, it should be because you have actively challenged and questioned why; you will have looked for any weakness in whatever the ritual seeks to buttress.

What We See

Ritual serves to satisfy a variety of human needs, such as those of inclusion, a sense of purpose and a clear hierarchy of status of the participants. There is nothing fundamentally wrong with a ritual as long as we are fully self-aware of what is actually being transacted. The greatest danger in a ritual is that an established ritual can switch minds off. We may be seduced into thinking that 'someone else is taking care of the thinking' or that 'the practices are perfectly reasonable or logical'. A ritual can take the place of open questions, and doubts might be dealt with falsely. The link between ritual and logic is the hijack point.

Ritual and logic have several important characteristics in common:

- They are both predictable.
- They do not change, they are consistent.
- They follow a known sequence.
- They follow agreed conventions.
- They can be reproduced by different people anywhere.
- Their outcome is always the same.
- People tend to trust both as equally correct and 'acceptable'.
- Both can become habitual, without much, if any, active thought.

Therein lies the greatest danger facing anyone, any group or any society.

Ritual Repetition and Security

If you are a parent and you have read your children stories, there comes a point in their lives at which they really enjoy hearing certain stories over and over again. There is a sense of security, a sort of being safe and in control because they know the pattern and the outcomes. Certainty allows them to 'safely' enjoy the story's journey from a position where they 'know' the pattern, the flow and the outcomes.

As adults, generally we continue to crave certainty, especially regarding important yet often uncertain aspects of our lives. In these elements of our lives we may be denied the clarity we have come to expect from logic. Because of this, we have a vulnerability that can be exploited by the seductive influence of ritual.

Ritual is seductive because it can provide a sense of certainty as a substitute for a gap in knowledge. There are lots of 'gaps' in our knowledge concerning who likes us, our real status, where we come from and where we are going. For example: if you say you love me, I can never know exactly what you actually feel, for how long you will feel this way or the depth or shallowness of your feeling. When we have to deal with questions to which there are no clear, unambiguous answers, we sometimes feel insecure. We want something or someone to close the gaps and give us certainty.

It is important to know the similarities between logical reasoning and ritual because when logical reason is thin or non-existent, a ritual may be used as a substitute to prevent people from thinking freely about their uncertainties.

Ritual is one of those subconscious triggers that switch our minds off and blind acceptance on. This is especially so if the rituals are very old. Ritual can therefore become a form of control over minds.

At a more mundane level, work is full of rituals: some petty, some egocentric, some adopted over the ages. Annual budget plans often follow an arcane ritual. If you want to make a difference by uprooting and replacing wrong rituals, this may mean fighting off an old guard that has a vested interest in keeping the 'old ways' going. Expect heavy resistance.

Ritual demands compliance of many and usually gives power to a few. To reinforce the power of the ritual, scale might be added. To ensure and retain control, fear and or force may also be included. Buildings, icons, processions and expense tend to get bigger to reflect the importance of the ritual and to buttress weak or difficult to verify 'truths'.

The size of the wedding reception and the number of guests are no guarantee that love will last any longer than it will. The imposing quality of the Enron head-office buildings conveyed an unjustified impression of strength and viability.

The pomp and precision of all the May Day processions through Moscow's Red Square in the twentieth century made no difference whatsoever to the viability of the communist USSR. Russian economic imbalances meant the communist system was ultimately doomed. The ritual of their annual arms display merely served to comfort a few and blinker many more.

Then there are the people of Easter Island who progressively built bigger statues to their dead ancestors. The ritual became so overwhelming that statue-building led to deforestation and an ecological disaster.

We have rituals for government, for giving honours, for judging and for taking life. Rituals are used to buttress something. Ritual provides a reassuring numbing effect because rituals mimic the pattern that logic follows. Some of the rituals may be rooted in established or handed-down wisdom to do with healthy living, survival or ordered societies. The danger in a ritual is the passage of time, because the majority of people in a society will, without thinking and without awareness, accept the convention set by a ritual, even if the outcome is unpalatable.

Our societies will always have a place for reassuring ritual, but as individuals we must be careful to question what we are being expected to believe. We must be very careful to remain genuinely self-aware. The danger of ritual is as an opiate. Ritual can create an illusion of certainty and security. A ritual demands social compliance and in so doing prevents free self-expression and may even demand suspension of everyday rational thought.

Groups of people need reassuring boundaries, agreeable laws and a measure of compliance to ensure social harmony. In return, the many protect the few and the few can enrich the many without arrogance. When valid routines exist they may order society but society remains free to question the process. A valid routine is not a ritual because it always remains open to question and change. These are very important distinctions. Institutions and societies need valid flexible routines in order to avoid unhealthy extremes. Once inflexible rituals are seen as the prevailing form of rule then the people with the controlling ideology eventually burn all books but their own and see new ideas as a threat.

What to Do

The single most important aspect of upgrading the way you think is self-awareness, and for this reason whenever a ritual is being enacted you should heighten your self-awareness and question everything.

Challenge the validity of a ritual – no matter how old it is. Does it still have a place and what is the ritual covering up or buttressing? Are we better off facing an uncertainty or is there a better way of dealing with the issue the ritual underpins? What illusion is being fostered?

If a ritual has been used in the past as a screen in front of non-rational decision-making, then get people used to the idea that some decisions need to be taken using their senses. Some decisions can only be taken based on a feeling. If this is the case, be explicit about the basis for your decision. Do not be afraid to explain that the basis of a decision is a feeling. Do not fear the uncertain nature of feelings compared to logic. Then get rid of the screen. Emotional decisions can be just as valid as any other, especially in highly ambiguous territory.

Uses

Questioning ritual. Keeping alive the freedom to think scientifically and philosophically without limitation AND to hold religious beliefs of your own. Some rituals are necessary and desirable for social cohesion.

Overuse

No matter how well-intentioned, a ritual can rob the power of the many and may result in an unhealthy concentration of power in the hands of a few 'keepers of the mystery'. Eventually, powerful people will seek to control that source of power as their own.

Module 78

Gut Feelings: Faith and the Truth

Any one of the following can lead
to a *personal* belief in a truth:
fact + fact
fact + agreed assumptions
a little feeling + fact
a lot of feeling + agreed assumptions
a lot of feeling + fact
a lot of feeling + another lot of feeling

We should not overlook the role of deeply held beliefs based on faith or deeply held emotions on how we think or interact with the world. For example, in crisis situations or where a decision is wanted despite incomplete information, we may turn to our 'gut instincts' to guide us. Our faith in someone or something might be formed in nanoseconds or after several years. Lifestyle, career and major commercial decisions can sometimes be taken based on 'feelings' or 'instincts'. We may well 'retro-justify' and create something in logic to mask a decision based upon an act of faith or something emotional, but if we do that we undermine our ability to learn how our feelings can guide us.

You need to be familiar with the way your mind deals with logical AND with faith-based/deeply emotional reasoning, because the rules and outcomes for each pattern are completely different. Self-awareness involves understanding whether your mind is using a logical or a deeply emotional pattern or a mixture of the two. You need to know how much 'head' and how much 'heart' guides your decisions and actions.

> *Despite our knowledge of biochemistry, matters of the heart defy the rules followed by logic.*

What We See

Our understanding process and the way we conclude what 'the truth is' can vary from person to person. We can arrive at our conclusions by a variety of routes. Of the various routes to forming a truth, one in particular – the logical, material, reasoning route – has become the major mental highway in Western society. Yet there are other significant ways through which we can form our beliefs in a truth or an estimate. For example, we can form our individual truths based upon experience as well as on our emotional sensations and feelings. A few patterns of 'sense-making' are illustrated above.

Feelings and Reason

When we employ logical, material reasoning we may arrive at a valuable conclusion or a belief. Conclusions formed in this way can travel easily to become widely accepted 'truths'. By this I mean 'truths' derived from conventional logic can be adopted by other people and reproduced without the originator. However, our thinking patterns involving deeply emotionally rooted issues such as faith, trust, love and forgiveness are different from those involving logic. Other people may have experiences of faith, trust, love and forgiveness but each individual experience will be unique and therefore cannot be codified and widely transferred so that other people experience exactly what the originator felt. We cannot codify or exactly transmit the truth of a feeling.

For example, my truth that I love someone **cannot be transferred** in any way similar to the transfer of something logical. Nor can love be easily or fully explained, since my sensation and experience of love is particular to me. Indeed, if my heart is broken and sometime later I fall in love again with someone new, the character and sensation of love could be quite a different experience. Nevertheless, I will still understand both relationships as 'being in love'. I do not, nor can I understand, love in a logical rational sense, but I do have faith that the feelings are very real.

My experience of love illustrates that the rules that guide logic do NOT translate to other parts of our sense-making process, nor should they. For example, in logic, one plus one is eternally two; however, one love plus another love is, sadly, not always equal to something eternal. Clearly you need to be aware of the difference between faith-based and rationally based judgements and decisions.

> When dealing with fast-changing volatile or ambiguous commercial or political situations, people may choose to be led by 'gut' instinct. This may well have proven effective in the past, but we should be conscious as to what sort of decision process is engaged. Sometimes an entrepreneur may 'sense' that a huge commercial opportunity is just over the horizon, out of sight of mere mortals. Far-sighted entrepreneurs may well be correct, but this is not always the case. The 'dot-com' crash at the turn of the last century provides many costly examples of such errors.

In practical terms, it can be dangerous to mix the sense-making patterns and rules regarding matters of the heart with matters of the logical mind. When arguments involving faith and reason clash, we compare cheese and chalk; it is not possible to mix the reasoning of one with the other. Yet they can exist side by side. The problem regarding issues of faith, love, trust and forgiveness is we cannot know for sure what goes on in another people's minds, nor can we accurately reproduce their thoughts and feelings. Any one person's experience of faith is unique and entirely internal to that one individual.

> The very public dispute in America between scientists and fundamentalist Christians over Darwin's theory of evolution and 'Intelligent Design' illustrates the clash of two distinct patterns of sense-making. The real problem with this contest is that each is challenging the very heart of the other's belief system. It is a common mistake for one group to believe that alternative views must compete head on. I believe that this discussion does **not** require an either/or decision. Both systems of belief can coexist as long as each sits in the right territory.
>
> It is very possible to have the two belief systems operating side by side – as long as we understand where they cannot be mixed. For example, scientists are allowed to have faith AND people who have faith are allowed also to logically question science. But it is not safe to use logic to question, validate or underpin faith, love, trust or forgiveness. Nor can science be advanced by substituting feelings in place of facts. At stake in this particular argument is the right to free thinking and free speech. The power of faith is within, is about what we feel, find and experience beyond what is logical. Faith, love, trust and forgiveness are deeply held, powerful **personal** truths.
>
> The arguments supporting faith are much more compelling when clerics stay on territory involving personal feelings, right philosophy, good conduct and spiritual well-being. The quality and transferability of faith-based reasoning collapses when people try to substitute fundamental science with what was wrongly believed to be true several thousand years ago. The world is not flat, nor was it ever so. We were given the power to think and to question. Now, as then, new scientific lessons do not necessarily have to undermine 'faith' – if you are aware, prepared to think impartially and prepared to tolerate some uncertainty within both systems of belief.

What to Do

It is up to you to find within yourself the matters that are not logical, that are faith-based or deeply emotional, such as love, faith, trust and forgiveness. Other people cannot 'give' forgiveness, love, faith or trust to you. These are uniquely personal feelings or beliefs **that you find**. Whilst matters of the heart may have some aspects in common **they are inconsistent** and *particular to the individual*. We could therefore reason that in regard to matters of the heart such as faith, love, trust, and forgiveness, these are *uniquely personal* and therefore non-transferable truths.

However, be aware that the two patterns of head and heart **can** coexist. Be aware of the basis of your decisions, whether head or heart. Be careful in matters regarding faith or emotion-based decisions. Because your faith or emotionally rooted beliefs *are particular to you*, these beliefs might be best used ONLY to guide your own path. These uniquely personal foundations *cannot be safely used* to guide groups of people because they are non-verifiable, are open to alternative interpretation and could be restated in alternative ways over time.

Some emotionally based decisions may be valid now, but their basis may evaporate over time. Therefore, regarding some emotionally based decisions, it is wise to have contingency plans in place to cover these possibilities.

Last Words

A world without love, trust, faith and forgiveness would be very cold indeed. Having sufficient courage to try to explain how you feel to people who may not feel what you feel, can be important and very effective, if used judiciously. Even more important, especially in a rarefied atmosphere, is to stay in touch with your own feelings, to honestly feel what you are feeling and not to defer or bury these till 'later'.

Remember all that remained within Pandora's box were hope, faith and charity. These are mankind's saviours and apply today, despite what your beliefs might be.

Your Relationship with Yourself

Module 79

Positive Attitudes and Beliefs

Success is commonly associated with a positive mind. Your starting point – a positive or negative perception of reality – strongly influences what you think and how you and others will act. A profoundly positive mindset is based on several factors, including security, preparedness, personal beliefs, philosophy and feelings.

What We See

If 'feelings' are off the agenda, then a positive mindset discussion will be a difficult, dry subject to deal with. Being positive is an enabling feeling but it needs to be genuine AND realistic. (Projecting a positive attitude despite unsound foundations might look odd.) When it comes to developing a positive mindset, as with many aspects of success, we are presented with another serial dilemma – a favourable balance has to be struck between several opposites. A successful positive frame might involve a slightly positive bias along several balances between:

- optimism vs realism (as opposed to cynicism)
- experimentation and curiosity vs caution and rigour
- fun vs sense
- go on that extra distance vs quit early and conserve resources
- fight again vs adapt to being beaten
- see the best in someone vs see the worst
- see the best in something vs see the worst in things
- joy vs anger and fear

If we get into the habit of looking in the right direction we can, with solid foundations, build an increasingly positive attitude. Some people pitch the balance to the negative and find reasons for not attempting to get what they want. Some pitch too far in one particular direction and end up appearing to be at odds with who they really are. A few people, however, are a real pleasure to meet and deal with. They are infectiously and authentically positive.

What to Do

Seek out and build nurturing experiences, people and ways of life that reinforce positive beliefs. Find a solid centre you can build on. Build and inhabit your own 'castles'.

'Walk Away' Preparation

Be prepared to walk away from ideas, people or situations that are not good, even if there is a personal cost involved. In practical terms, it's a good idea to be prepared long in advance to do a 'walk away' and have sufficient resources and choices to allow you to do this at **a time of your choosing**. Your self-confidence rises knowing that you are prepared. You create your own security. When you know you have the potential to walk away, your ability to speak honestly about what is happening rises significantly. People respect you if you are socially skilled enough to speak clearly and truthfully. A virtuous circle of building positive attitude and self-confidence then arises.

Preparation for Your Move Forward

If you cannot do what you want to do now, then get ready for the day when you will. Keep notes about what you will do. Build skills and alliances. Begin by at least thinking about and then taking a few easy steps forward toward your ideal and stay on that journey till it pays off.

Authenticity and Confidence

A positive attitude can be formed but it has to be authentic to work for you. You need to be true to yourself. In order to do that you need to, understand who you are: your philosophy and your beliefs and values. If you cannot be true to yourself, how will you represent yourself to others in an honest and convincing way? Building confidence is about getting yourself totally aligned. Your beliefs, thoughts, feelings, actions and reactions all need to feed back to say, 'Yes this is right,' and other people should confirm that what you are doing is true, worthy and right. These principles apply just as much to an organisation.

Doing the Right Thing

Self-confidence and a positive attitude are built up from firm personal foundations. Our deepest personal foundations are within our frames of reference and are hard-wired to our feelings. Remember, our feelings are super-fast mental circuits that can override conscious thought AND behaviour. So to be confident, our deepest feelings have to be in line with what we are thinking and doing. If deep down you feel something is wrong, your feelings can and will hijack the flow of what you are trying to do. An enduring positive attitude has to be built on a firm self-belief that what you are doing is the right thing. This cannot be the case if what you are doing is rejected

227

by your conscience or by self-doubt. Occasionally, the law of the land is open to interpretation, but a higher moral law is not. Moral law should not be forgotten.

'It is an old wisdom that there is no freedom except under the law. Freedom without law is licence, which soon turns to anarchy and shortly thereafter into tyranny.'

Peter F. Drucker.

If there are doubts or uncertainties created from bad ethical or unsound decisions in the past, then long-term confidence will be undermined. It is necessary to set your conscience right with the past, seek forgiveness or put right what is wrong and then move on. Remember, no human lives a perfect, error-free life, so we must be ready to forgive others and ourselves in order to progress.

> *Forgiveness is part of the confidence-building process.*
> *Deal with the past, correct, repair, forgive and move forward.*

Ethics

A successful person or organisation needs sound foundations – rotten roots do not form healthy plants. The thoughts and intentions behind the actions must be sound too. Strong ethics are a must.

> *The Russians have a saying: 'A fish rots from the head first.'*

In running a deep check on the quality of your foundations for confidence look as much to your own ethics as you do to those above you. If there is any rot it must be cut out and cast away so that a clean beginning can be made to build confidence. If your community or organisation does not foster positive beliefs, then start with your own beliefs and create a genuinely new positive story to lead with.

Here is the simplest set of ethical guidelines shared with me by an Indian scholar. I was told these three simple precepts are over 7,000 years old. They will guide you in most things in life:

- think good thoughts
- say good things
- do good things

If what you do meets these three tests in the eyes of millions of common people from different cultures, then you are on a good path.

Feelings

A positive frame of mind involves a humane feeling. Feelings need to be acknowledged if this force is to be harnessed for the good. If the feeling is sensed as positive but lacks humanity, then it is probably blind ambition, lust or greed.

Why This Is Important

Positive thinking and positive action involve the emotions. Our emotions are hard-wired to our deepest beliefs. What we believe steers our perception and what we do. Many things will happen to us in our lives that are beyond our control; however, we CAN choose how to interpret what we find and we CAN choose how to act. Our choices, whether positive or negative, will determine our success and well-being. These choices are enabled once we have sorted out who we are, our philosophies and our preparedness. A positive attitude from a position of confidence and strength is preferable for us as individuals and for us as a species.

TIPS

- In seeking the right way for yourself, avoid prescriptive 'off the shelf', easy answers.
- We are human: we make mistakes. That is how we learn. Forgive and move on.
- Take wisdom from wherever it springs.
- Wise people are fallible and make mistakes too. So don't set anyone up as a 'guru'.
- Be your own wise person – think things through for yourself.

Uses

High performance, happiness, well-being and fulfilment. Doing the right thing. Creating lasting institutions and ideas. Setting up guidelines for decision-making in the absence of authority.

Next Steps

Even if you are not inclined toward religion, it can be a good idea to read different religious texts to gather the wisdom of the ages. You still have a choice in what ideas to accept or reject.

Winning Philosophies

Module 80

Shared Winning Philosophy

Reached the top and still
not in control!

It is a mistake to assume that you can achieve complete control. 'Power and control' are an illusion.

People enjoy a sense of direction and being well led **BUT** they often **also** want the freedom to choose what they will do. There may therefore be a dilemma regarding how we work best.

What We See

People want self-determination, yet there are occasions when a clear sense of control is desirable; for example, during a crisis, or in the safe landing of an aircraft. In a crisis, people are often predisposed to align behind a leader and will cede control until the crisis passes. Retaining control by creating a constant state of crisis is neither sensible nor healthy – you're likely to end up with a neurotic outfit or nation state.

Most meaningful long-term endeavours become successful when people's 'hands, hearts and minds' collaborate: when many things are connected, often in subtle ways. Not enough control and there is the risk of chaos; however, too much control turns people off. Furthermore, excessive control gets in the way of people forming great connections between new ideas, new processes and new contacts.

An excellent example that shows inspired leadership thinking, despite intense pressure, comes from Richard Branson, head of Virgin Airlines. He faced a crisis in which the airline travel industry was almost totally becalmed during the first Gulf War. His airline needed to remain solvent despite an almost total lack of passengers. Richard told his staff he didn't know what to do for the best. Making people redundant wasn't an option, he said. Instead of telling the staff the answer, he allowed them to provide the solution – unpaid leave for as long as it took. He did not exercise the narrow version of 'control', involving command and direction. Instead his 'power' comes from letting go and trusting his people. My interpretation is that employees reflected back to him the faith he had consistently demonstrated in his workforce.

What makes Branson's diverse empire successful is a combination of several forces that include great ideas backed up by great followers; in other words, great connections between people and ideas, and a shared, 'can do', positive philosophy. That positive environment is no accident. Richard's thousands upon thousands of staff are connected to him AND to the ideals of their company. The power of Richard Branson is that he is not in control. He sets the tone and shares the controls. People have faith in him and what he stands for. In other words he has crafted a 'winning philosophy' that travels in terms of brand and employee performance.

Julian Richer of the UK's Richer Sounds; Ricardo Semler of Semco; 3M; and Johnson & Johnson all adopted winning philosophies that created lasting winning behaviours in very large numbers of people.

Winning is clearly based on how people think.

What to Do

You can adopt a winning philosophy whether you own an organisation or not. Realise that control is for a crisis only; the rest of the time there is competition for 'control'. In order to reconcile competition for control, look at a third option. Drop 'who controls' for 'what controls' in the form of a shared set of agreed reference points and ideals. These might be described as a shared philosophy or a set of values. Whatever it is called, this third 'higher order' guides everyone's decisions. When a higher order of control is in place people tend to do 'the right thing' at the right time. Leadership, team playing and corporate citizenship are all a matter of shaping and upholding a winning philosophy. If the right beliefs are not there you can begin to create or negotiate them.

Leadership and citizenship are then a matter for creating and managing 'climates' and shared belief systems. Consider what people really want and then try and deliver against that. Not everyone will want the same thing so obviously this is not an easy thing to accomplish. People's needs change over time, so keep checking. If you are a leader make sure what you believe is followed through at all levels at all times – from top to bottom. Junior people must be allowed to challenge and manage upwards within the safety and protection of the agreed values.

> *Johnson & Johnson have a credo. It is worth reading because this is a living, working document. Their credo has helped steer a massive, highly diversified organisation to consistent success for decades. Any business decision has to match up to the credo and I know that junior managers can and do challenge their bosses with a 'credo challenge' when they believe the credo might be stretched in the wrong direction.*

Why This Is Important

When there is no one to turn to and you know you have to make a right and honest decision, then socially agreed principles will guide you. A winning philosophy is one of several important elements within a series of balanced dilemmas that must be managed in any complex organisation.

> *Social 'norms' are much more powerful than old-fashioned command and control. Passion, interest and excitement are powerful forces people can bring to their work for free – if you let them.*

When there is an excellent alignment of many good people, great things happen. What is visible in a successful situation tends to be accounted for rationally and in terms of material resources. Despite this, other groups of people with the very same materials may fail to match the same level of success. A vital yet often 'invisible' ingredient for success comes from the way people align their hearts and minds in an irresistible alliance to achieve shared, higher goals. This whole success cascade stems from positive:

- attitude
- alignment of clearly understood values and ethics
- action consistent with agreed values

The manner in which people think, believe, share and agree their actions is the crux of the matter.

TIPS

- Telling people what their values are going to be just won't work. Neither will well-intentioned poster campaigns. All levels of management need to behave consistently with what is agreed and, without exception, need to be rebuked or dismissed if they fail.
- Manage the context in which people operate – take care of the rules rather than the specifics. Individuals will decide what needs to be done within the rules and the contexts you set.
- Create stories that will last and that will ripple through your organisation.
- Be creative AND uphold your values, especially in a crisis.
- Reaching 'the top' is a matter of collaborating at a higher level. Control is a vain ambition.

Uses

A set of values guides difficult decisions, especially those involving dilemmas. Values, guidelines and philosophies set the boundaries within which great decisions can be created and upheld. Useful in a crisis. A shared philosophy helps people to make good decisions quickly on behalf of others.

Overuse

Contemplating the number of angels that can be fitted on a pinhead. Whilst bad decisions might be avoided, a good working philosophy cannot always differentiate between two or more good decisions. Additional navel gazing or introspection is not productive – good judgement *as well as* timely action remain important.

Next Steps

Research the skills and practices necessary to manage climates; for example, consider a storytelling exploration.

Author's Note

This is an area I am interested in continuing to develop. If you have something you would like to share with me concerning a culture or a working philosophy, please contact me via the web site **http://www.spreid.com**

Module 81

Two-edged Sword

There is a simple masterful philosophy concerning a two-edged sword. One edge is as fine and sharp as the other. One is used to cut, implying action when necessary; but the other is merely held and things fall upon the sword involving no effort on your part. This implies masterful action alongside masterful inaction. This is an interesting pairing, worth remembering.

Module 82

Going Full Circle: innocence

Earlier in this book, I suggested that we are born with a blank slate. As we reach higher levels of consciousness to help us cope with this complex life, we may find ourselves in search of the state of mind we knew as innocent children. We seek simple innocence and openness; however, there is no fast track. The pains and the gains of living cannot be avoided. But once we find innocence and openness, the opportunity to see the world without the veils of experience or illusion is a blessing available to anyone. Artists and philosophers hope they will find this sort of innocence but are aware that the act of actually trying calls in experience and therefore prevents them from experiencing what they want. Not wanting but being ready to accept the innocence as it arrives, is the way.

Next Steps

It can be helpful to read a range of philosophy books (see below). Try attending philosophy workshops. Some military textbooks on warfare develop a variety of insights into dealing with very difficult fast-moving dilemmas, although I do find books like this quite difficult and unpleasant reading. Travel widely and look beyond the filter of first impressions.

Further Reading

An easy-to-read, pleasant and surprisingly practical book I can strongly recommend is *The Consolations of Philosophy*, by Alain de Botton. I can also strongly recommend the essays and books by Krishnamurti; *The Art of War*, by Sun Tzu (written circa 500 BC); *The Prince*, by Machiavelli; and *The Prophet*, by Khalil Gibran. Charles Handy's books are all worth reading. Bertrand Russell provides a compendium of easy-to-read digests of many different belief systems adopted over the last few thousand years in *A History of Western Philosophy*.

An Eastern perspective is useful too. Buddhism is a philosophy with no deity. You might wish to consider looking into books on Tao – or 'The Way'. The work does contain useful, if often oblique, guidelines created from an alternative perspective.

Last Words

There is no one single-trick model, skill or tool that will make you a smarter person. There are in fact many things you need to bring into play at the same time. This book provides over 80 tools and over 200 tips on how you can acquire and practise a range of different skills so that you get more out of life.

But for smart people it doesn't end here:

- You'll want to know what happened (good or bad) and to learn and improve from each experience.
- You'll want to share this information and to spread the learning widely to those who matter.
- You'll want to do better next time or to make things easier, even if this time your actions were 'enough'.
- You'll want to know if your actions have made material changes to the who and how you are.
- You'll want to know if you are still fit for the future.

In other words,
being self-aware,
you will continue to learn.

And Finally

A Story of Two Fools

I once had to run a meeting where I knew one of the young delegates had an extremely low opinion of me. So I started the team meeting by saying, 'There are two fools. One believes everything I say and the other believes absolutely nothing I say. Please discuss why they are fools.'

It worked. I mention this here because this simple tale demonstrates the dangers of a closed mind and of unthinking acceptance. It is a useful exercise because the conclusions suggest we can even learn from those we think to be fools and that we would be foolish not to. The two fools story I concocted also shows just how fallible we all are.

Each of us should be sufficiently self-aware to think for ourselves and to judge whether or not we accept what other people say.

*With this in mind, if you spot any sort of error in my book or if you can suggest an alternative way of thinking something through or if you have real-life examples that you think would help future readers, I would be very pleased to hear from you! Please contact me via my publisher or via **http://www.spreid.com***

I hope my book will help you on your own personal journey and that you will in turn be willing to help me.

If you found my book useful, please encourage five other people to buy:

High Performance **Thinking Skills**

In a Hurry

Which Modules to Use for Specific Subjects

Each module is concise and usually less than four pages long

Below are my recommendations as to which combination of ideas, models and tools might help you address a specific issue. In many of the subjects listed I would generally recommend reading the whole book.

In a fast, demanding world I am increasingly aware that people want their information in a quick and concise way. With this in mind, most modules are comprised of just three or four pages. Additional material is available to supplement many of the modules via the author's web site: see **http://www.spreid.com**. Quite a few of the modules have multiple applications and can work for you under a variety of different circumstances.

Generally speaking, the **higher numbers refer** to tools for use where there are **higher levels of difficulty**. Occasionally the numbers listed below do not run sequentially.

Key Models

These apply in many situations. Several of these models work in combination with each other. The baseline models that recur most often can be found within modules 1, 14, 15, 19, **22**, 25, 26 and 32. If you only read one module from my book, I suggest you read module 22.

Strategy Development

A lot of strategy is often dealt with in a dull linear way and often lacks foresight or imagination. Discover alternative ways of thinking rationally and non-rationally about the future. See modules 1, 2, 11 to 15, 19, 22, 25, 26, 34, 39 to 42, 47, 49, 50, 51, 58, 63, 64, 70, 72, 80, 81.

Dealing with Change

If you cannot cope with change then you will suffer. Learn some practical ways of thinking about and dealing effectively with change. See modules 1, 2, 10, 14, 15, 19 to 23, 25, 28 to 32, 35, 36, 37, 40, 42, 47, 48, 49, 52, 57 to 61, 66, 68, 73, 79.

Leadership Ability

There is no one right way to manage and lead people. In order to perform well, you need a range of abilities and tools to guide you through a range of difficult situations. See how in modules 1, 2, 10, 16 to 22, 26, 32, 35, 39, 41 to 48, 57 to 60, 66, 71, 75, 76, 79, 80.

Innovation and Creativity

Playful thinking is very productive if channelled toward pragmatic decisions. I have successfully led several thousand people through thinking skills transfer workshops. Learn some of the lessons in how to be more creative and how to open your mind to new possibilities. Read modules 1 to 9, 14, 15, 18, 19, 22, 25, 26, 33, 34, 40, 47, 72.

Managing the Balance Between Work and Real Life

We all talk about 'chilling out' or 'escaping to a better life' – *later*. Do it now! Take a big look at how you live your life, consider what you are doing to your body and mind and decide how you will get the most out of life, in a healthy way. See modules 32, 21 to 23, 35 to 37, 48, 57, 71, 73, 79.

Ambiguity, Uncertainty, Certainty and Risk

The most interesting parts of life are not logical. So how do we deal with reality when things become foggy? Read these modules to find out: 49, 51, 53, 25, 35, 62, 42, 43 and 47.

Truth and Relative Truth

The 'truth' isn't always what you thought it was. Get a grip on reality and how other people shape it. Read modules 15, 22 to 25, 28 to 31, 53, 54, 76 to 78.

Error

Many people think of error as a bad thing. That is not a smart attitude. Learn how error can sometimes be a good thing. Error is normal. The following modules can help you: 15, 25, 40, 41, 47.

Problem-solving and Decision-making

There are all sorts, shapes and sizes of problems. Discover how each type can lead to a different outcome in modules 16, 17, 38, 39, 42, 62 to 65, 74, 75, 78.

Negotiation

A great deal of our lives is spent negotiating for what we want. Here are a number of tips and tools that will help you: 1, 10, 2, 14, 15, 21, 22, 25, 33, 34, 36, 39, 47, 68, 69, 71. Also see the section on conflict.

Relationships

The most complicated aspect of life involves relationships with other people. Find practical tips, models and guidelines that can help you here: 22, 1, 14, 15, 16, 17, 21, 42, 47, 48, 66 to 69, 79, 80.

Conflict

Tips, tools and models to help you deal with conflict: 22, 1, 10, 14 to 18, 20, 21, 25, 47, 57, 58, 60, 61, 69

Managing Your Career

People sometimes spend more time thinking about their next holiday than where they are going with their lives. Think about your life. See modules 22, 32, 36, 15, 21, 25, 35, 42, 48, 71, 73, 76, 80, 81, 57 to 60.

Philosophy and Personal Performance

What you deeply believe will profoundly impact the way you perform. If the way you are living your life lines up well with what you believe, then you have a chance to feel fulfilled. So what do you 'believe'? What is your personal philosophy? See modules 22, 23, 24, 48, 70, 71, 80, 81, 82, 76 to 78, and start to find out for yourself.

Coping with a Complex Life

Please read the whole book.

More detailed developer and trainer notes plus additional exercises and guidelines are available via the author's web site.

Visit http://www.spreid.com

Overview by General Subject Heading

Upgrade Your Models and Tools

Territory 1 see modules 2 to 9 then 10 to 13
Territory 2 see modules 25 to 32
Territory 3 see modules 49 to 56
Territory 4 see module 72

Tuning the Controls

Territory 1 see modules 14 and 15 then 24
Territory 2 see modules 33 to 37
Territory 3 see modules 57 to 61
Territory 4 see module 73

Decisions

Territory 1 see modules 16 and 17
Territory 2 see modules 38 to 41
Territory 3 see modules 62 to 65
Territory 4 see modules 74 and 75

Feeling and Thinking

Territory 1 see modules 18 to 20
Territory 2 see modules 42 to 46
Territory 3 see modules 66 and 67
Territory 4 see modules 76 to 78

Relationships and Reality

Territory 1 see module 21
Territory 2 see module 47
Territory 3 see modules 68 and 69
Territory 4 see module 79

Winning Philosophies

Territory 1 see modules 22 and 23
Territory 2 see module 48
Territory 3 see modules 70 and 71
Territory 4 see modules 80, 81, 82